MODERN INDONESIA

The Postwar World
General Editors: A. J. Nicholls and Martin S. Alexander

As distance puts events into perspective, and as evidence accumulates, it begins to be possible to form an objective historical view of our recent past. *The Postwar World* is an ambitious series providing a scholarly but readable account of the way our world has been shaped in the crowded years since the Second World War. Some volumes deal with regions, or even single nations, others with important themes; all are written by expert historians drawing on the latest scholarship as well as their own research and judgements. The series should be particularly welcome to students, but it is designed also for the general reader with an interest in contemporary history.

Decolonization in Africa Second Edition   *J. D. Hargreaves*

The Community of Europe: A History of European Integration since 1945, Second Edition   *Derek W. Urwin*

Northern Ireland since 1945   *Sabine Wichert*

A History of Social Democracy in Postwar Europe   *Stephen Padgett and William E. Paterson*

'The Special Relationship': A Political History of Anglo-American Relations since 1945   *C. J. Bartlett*

Rebuilding Europe: Western Europe, America and Postwar Reconstruction   *D. W. Ellwood*

The Pacific Basin since 1945: A History of The Foreign Relations of the Asian, Australasian and American Rim States and the Pacific Islands *Roger C. Thompson*

The Bonn Republic: West German Democracy 1945-1990   *A. J. Nicholls*

Central Europe since 1945   *Paul G. Lewis*

International Relations since 1945. A History in Two Volumes
John Dunbabin
   The Cold War: The Great Powers and their Allies
   The Post-Imperial Age: The Great Powers and the Wider World

Modern Indonesia: A history since 1945
Robert Cribb and Colin Brown

Peace Movements: International Protest and World Politics since 1945
April Carter

Modern Indonesia

A history since 1945

Robert Cribb and Colin Brown

Longman
London and New York

Addison Wesley Longman Limited,
Edinburgh Gate,
Harlow, Essex CM20 2JE, England
and Associated Companies throughout the world.

*Published in the United States of America
by Addison Wesley Longman, New York*

First published 1995
Second impression 1997

ISBN 0 582 05712 4 CSD
ISBN 0 582 05713 2 PPR

British Library Cataloguing-in-Publication Data

A catalogue record for this book is
available from the British Library

Library of Congress Cataloging-in-Publication Data
Cribb, R. B.
    Modern Indonesia : a history since 1945 / Robert Cribb and Colin
Brown.
        p.   cm. — (Postwar world)
    Includes bibliographical references and index.
    ISBN 0–582–05712–4. — ISBN 0–582–05713—2 (pbk.)
    1. Indonesia—History—1945– I. Brown, Colin. II. Title.
III. Series.
DS644.C44   1995
959.803—dc20   94–48236
                                                                         CIP

Set by 5B in 10/12 pt Baskerville
Produced by Longman Singapore Publishers (Pte) Ltd.
Printed in Singapore

Contents

Glossary

aksi sepihak	unilateral actions by the PKI to implement land reform in the Javanese countryside in 1963–64.
Apodeti	(Associação Populár Democrática Timorense) Timorese Popular Democratic Association: small, pro-Indonesian political party in East Timor.
ASDT	(Associação Social Democrática Timorense) Timorese Social Democratic Association, left-wing forerunner to Fretilin.
ASEAN	Association of Southeast Asian Nations.
asli	indigenous.
azas tunggal	sole guiding principle; the Pancasila was given this status for all mass organisations in 1978, though it was not enforced until 1985.
Badan Kerja Sama	Cooperative Bodies: mass organisations affiliated with the army under Guided Democracy.
BAKIN	(Badan Koordinasi Intelijen Negara) State Board for Intelligence Coordination.
Baperki	(Badan Permusyawaratan Kewarganegaraan Indonesia) Consultative Body on Indonesian Citizenship: predominantly *peranakan* Chinese political organisation which argued for the right of Chinese Indonesians to retain their culture.
BAPPENAS	(Badan Perencanaan Pembangunan Nasional) National Development Planning Board.
barisan	front or brigade (used by both political and irregular military organisations).

BFO	(Bijeenkomst voor Federaal Overleg) Federal Consultative Assembly.
Cukong	somewhat critical term for Chinese Indonesian businesspeople enjoying a close economic relationship with senior government figures.
Darul Islam	'The Realm of Islam': a rebellion in many parts of Indonesia in the 1950s and 1960s aiming to create an Islamic state.
dasar negara	basis of the state.
Dharma Wanita	Lit. 'The Duty of Women': the compulsory association of wives of civil servants.
DPR	(Dewan Perwakilan Rakyat) People's Representative Council.
dwifungsi	dual function: right and duty of the military to oversee the state; military involvement in politics and government.
formateur	one responsible for negotiating the make-up of a cabinet.
Fretilin	(Frente Revolucionária do Timor Leste Independente) Revolutionary Front for an Independent East Timor.
GBHN	(Garis Besar Haluan Negara) Broad Outlines of State Policy.
Giyugun	Japanese-sponsored Indonesian military units (mainly in Sumatra).
Golkar	Initially a federation of army-sponsored associations and trade unions, with the name Sekretariat Bersama Golongan Karya (Joint Secretariat of Functional Groups); later the main electoral vehicle for the government under the New Order; eventually came to resemble a political party.
Guided Democracy	President Sukarno's semi-dictatorial rule of Indonesia from 1957 to 1965.
Hankamrata	(Pertahanan dan Keamanan Rakyat Semesta) Total People's Defence and Security.
HMI	(Himpunan Mahasiswa Islam) Muslim Students Association.
IGGI	Inter-Governmental Group on Indonesia.
IPKI	(Ikatan Pendukung Kemerdekaan Indonesia) League of the Defenders of Indonesian

	Independence: a small army-based political party.
ISDV	(Indische Sociaal-Democratische Vereeniging) Indies Social Democratic Association.
kabupaten	district, regency.
KAMI	(Kesatuan Aksi Makasiswa Indonesia) Indonesian Students Action Front.
Kejawen	traditional Javanese religion, nominally Islamic but blending Hindu and animist beliefs and practices with those of Islam.
keterbukaan	political openness.
KNIL	(Koninklijk Nederlandsch Indisch Leger) Royal Netherlands Indies Army.
KNIP	(Komite Nasional Indonesia Pusat) Central Indonesian National Committee: quasi-parliament 1945–49.
konsepsi	concept: used by Sukarno to foreshadow the ideas underlying Guided Democracy.
KOPKAMTIB	(Komando Operasi Pemulihan Keamanan dan Ketertiban) Operational Command for the Restoration of Security and Order.
Korpri	(Korps Pegawai Republik Indonesia) Civil Servants Corps of the Republic of Indonesia: the compulsory Civil Service Association.
KOSTRAD	(Komando Tjadangan Strategis Angkatan Darat) Army Strategic Reserve Command.
KOTI	(Komando Operasi Tertinggi) Supreme Operational Command (for the liberation of West Irian).
kyai	rural Islamic teachers.
Linggajati Agreement	reached between Indonesian and Dutch negotiators at Linggajati, West Java, in November 1946; it provided for a federal Indonesia within a Dutch-Indonesian Union.
Malari	(Malapetaka Limabelas Januari) Disaster of 15 January (1974): riots in Jakarta, ostensibly against the visiting Japanese prime minister Kakuei Tanaka but prompted by concern over corruption, abuse of power and uneven development in Indonesia.
marhaen	ordinary poor but property-owning Indonesian.
marhaenism	doctrine of social responsibility to poor Indonesians.

Masjumi	modernist Muslim party.
modernism	that stream within Islam which emphasises the Qur'an (Koran) and the teachings of Muhammad rather than the interpretations of Islamic scholars.
MPR	(Majelis Permusyawaratan Rakyat) People's Consultative Assembly.
MPRS	(Majelis Permusyawaratan Rakyat Sementara) Provisional People's Consultative Assembly.
mufakat	decision-making by consensus.
Murba	small Marxist party hostile to the PKI.
musyawarah	deliberation and discussion involving all parties to an issue.
NASAKOM	(Nasionalisme, Agama, Komunisme) Nationalism, Religion, Communism: Indonesia's national ideology as formulated by President Sukarno under Guided Democracy.
Nefos	New Emerging Forces
NEKOLIM	neo-colonialists, colonialists and imperialists.
New Order	the political system under President Suharto, characterised by economic development and political restriction.
NU	(Nahdatul Ulama) Islamic Scholars Party.
Oldefos	Old Established Forces.
OPM	(Organisasi Papua Merdeka) Free Papua Movement.
OPSUS	(Operasi Khusus) Special Operations.
Pancasila	Five Principles: Belief in God, National Unity, Humanitarianism, People's Sovereignty, Social Justice and Prosperity. They were devised by Sukarno in July 1945 shortly before the declaration of independence to identify the basic beliefs which united all Indonesians despite their other cultural and ideological differences. Under Suharto's New Order, the Pancasila became for a time the ideological vehicle for a corporatist state.
Parkindo	(Partai Kristen Indonesia): Protestant Party.
Parmusi	(Partai Muslimin Indonesia): short-lived successor party to Masjumi.
Partai Katolik	Catholic Party.

PDI	(Partai Demokrasi Indonesia) Indonesian Democratic Party.
pembangunan	development.
pemuda	youth.
peranakan	ethnic Chinese whose primary cultural orientation is to Indonesia, not China.
Permesta	(Piagam Perjuangan Semesta Alam) Charter of Universal Struggle.
Perti	(Persatuan Tarbiyah Islamiyah) Islamic Education Association: an orthodox Muslim political party.
PETA	(Pembela Tanah Air) (Army of) the Defenders of the Homeland: Indonesian auxiliary army units established by the Japanese on Java.
petrus	*penembakan misterius* mysterious shootings: a government-sponsored campaign to assassinate known criminals, beginning 1982.
PIR	(Partai Indonesia Raja) Greater Indonesia Party.
PKI	(Partai Komunis Indonesia) Indonesian Communist Party.
PNI	(Partai Nasional Indonesia) Indonesian Nationalist Party.
PPKI	(Panitia Persiapan Kemerdekaan Indonesia) Preparatory Committee for Indonesian Independence.
PPP	(Partai Persatuan Pembangunan) Unity Development Party: officially approved Muslim party created in 1973 by the compulsory merger of existing Muslim parties.
PRC	People's Republic of China.
priyayi	traditional elite of Java.
PRN	(Partai Rakjat Nasional) National People's Party.
PRRI	(Pemerintah Revolusioner Republik Indonesia) Revolutionary Government of the Republic of Indonesia.
PSI	(Partai Sosialis Indonesia) Indonesian Socialist Party.
PSII	(Partai Sarekat Islam Indonesia) Islamic Association Party of Indonesia: a radical Muslim party.

Renville Agreement	reached between Indonesian and Dutch negotiators aboard the USS *Renville* in Jakarta Bay.
RIS	(Republik Indonesia Serikat) officially translated as Republic of the United States of Indonesia but better rendered as Federal Republic of Indonesia.
RMS	(Republik Maluku Selatan) Republic of the South Moluccas.
Round Table Conference	the negotiations in 1949 which led to the final transfer of sovereignty in the archipelago from the Netherlands to Indonesia.
RUSI	Republic of the United States of Indonesia.
transmigration	the programme of shifting people from the densely populated islands of Java and Bali to less densely populated islands.
UDT	(União Democrática Timorense) Timorese Democratic Union.
uleëbalang	traditional aristocracy in Aceh, north Sumatra.
Volksraad	People's Council: a quasi-legislative assembly created by the Dutch in Indonesia in 1918.

Editorial Foreword

The aim of this series is to describe and analyse the history of the World since 1945. History, like time, does not stand still. What seemed to many of us only recently to be 'current affairs' or the stuff of political speculation, has now become material for historians. The editors feel that it is time for a series of books which will offer the public judicious and scholarly, but at the same time readable, accounts of the way in which our present-day world has been shaped since the Second World War. The period which began in 1945 has witnessed political events and socio-economic developments of enormous significance for the human race, as important as anything which happened before Hitler's death or the bombing of Hiroshima. Ideologies have waxed and waned, the industrial economies have boomed and bust, empires of various types have collapsed, new nations have emerged and sometimes themselves fallen into decline. While we can be thankful that no major armed conflict occurred between the so-called superpowers, there have been many other wars, and terrorism emerged as an international plague. Although the position of ethnic minorities improved in some countries, it worsened dramatically in others. As communist tyrannies relaxed their grip on many areas of the world, so half-forgotten national conflicts re-emerged. Nearly everywhere the status of women became an issue which politicians were unable to avoid. The same was true of the global environment, apparent threats to which have been a recurrent source of international concern. These are only some of the developments we hope will be illuminated by this series as it unfolds.

The books in the series will not follow any set pattern; they will vary in length according to the needs of the subject. Some will deal with regions, or even single nations, and others with themes. Not all of them will begin in 1945, and the terminal date may vary; as with the length, the time-span chosen will be appropriate to the question under discussion. All the books, however, will be written by expert historians drawing on the latest research, as well as their own expertise and judgement. The series should be particularly welcome to students, but it is designed also for the general reader with an interest in contemporary history. We hope that the books will stimulate scholarly discussion and encourage specialists to look beyond their own particular interests to engage in wider controversies.

History, and especially the history of the recent past, is neither 'bunk' nor an intellectual form of stamp-collecting, but an indispensable part of an educated person's approach to life. If it is not written by historians it will be written by others of a less discriminating and more polemical disposition. The editors are confident that this series will help to ensure the victory of the historical approach, with consequential benefits for its readers.

A.J. Nicholls
Martin S. Alexander

Preface

This book arose out of a course in Indonesian politics which we taught together in the School of Modern Asian Studies (now Faculty of Asian and International Studies) at Griffith University in Brisbane, Australia in the mid-1980s. We were not satisfied then with the bulk of the books we recommended our students to read. There was not much that was contemporary in its orientation, rigorous in its treatment of the subject matter and yet accessible to students in style and format. This book is an attempt to remedy these shortcomings. It adopts a largely thematic approach to recent Indonesian history, trying to develop and follow through ideas rather than personalities or the chronology of events. We have tried out both the general approach and specific sections of the book on our students – at Griffith University initially but subsequently the Universities of Tasmania and Queensland, and Flinders University – and modified both in the light of their responses. We are indebted to them for their criticism of the text, and have tried to make many of the amendments they suggested.

The book has also benefited from the critical comments of colleagues at the various Universities at which we have taught, and of the publisher's readers, for which we thank them.

As with all such work, though, the ultimate responsibility for the content of the book, and all errors of fact and of interpretation rest with us. We would like however to think that, given the number of people who have had a hand in shaping the text one way or another, the burden is fairly light.

As all who have done it will know, teaching collaboratively with colleagues, and then writing with them, can put a strain on even the most valued of relationships. Our experience was no different, but we are grateful that we have come out of the exercise with our friendship intact. Nonetheless, while naturally we welcome comments from readers of this book, both teachers and students, we hope it will be a year or so before a revised edition becomes necessary.

CHAPTER ONE

The Origins of Modern Indonesia

Two hundred years ago, the Indonesian nation did not exist. The sprawling archipelago between the Australian and Asian mainlands was divided amongst Dutch, British and Portuguese colonialists and an array of independent indigenous states of varying size and power. Nor was there a sense of Indonesian identity among the people of the archipelago, then numbering perhaps five million. They were divided into 200 or more distinct ethnic groups, ranging from fiercely Muslim Acehnese on the northern tip of Sumatra and the Catholic communities of Flores and Timor to the Hindu Balinese and the animist tribes of the interior of Kalimantan (Borneo)[1] and New Guinea, as well as more recent immigrant communities such as Chinese in western Kalimantan and Europeans in the cities of Java.

Indonesia came into being because the Dutch, expelling or confining their European rivals and subduing the indigenous states one by one, imposed a degree of political unity on the archipelago and created an expansive colonial state called the Netherlands Indies. Dutch domination not only created an archipelago-wide state but also transformed the social and economic fabric of the indigenous societies, eventually creating a sense of grievance and crisis which culminated in a successful campaign to end Dutch colonialism and to transform the colonial state into the independent state of Indonesia. The turbulent politics of the

---

1. Many Indonesian names for places in the archipelago differ slightly or completely from the commonly-known Western names. In general, we have preferred modern Indonesian terminology, with Western names in brackets, except when there is a good historical reason for retaining the Western name.

1

Indonesian Republic began with independence in 1945, but to understand the passions, the ideals and the bitterness which have driven those politics, it is necessary to turn first to the experience of its people before independence.

History has fractured the 13,000 islands of the Indonesian archipelago in many ways. To begin with, the vast majority of today's Indonesians are descended from two distinct ethnic groups. Six thousand years ago, much of the archipelago was inhabited by scattered small communities of dark-skinned, curly-haired Melanesian peoples of whom relatively little is known. About 4000 BC, the archipelago was invaded by a people from the north, Austronesians from the island of Taiwan with paler skins and straight hair, who brought the technology of pottery, bows and arrows and outrigger canoes. The newcomers swept through the region, sometimes driving out, sometimes absorbing the Melanesians. Some pushed on in time to Madagascar, off the African coast; others pressed out into the Pacific to become the ancestors of today's Polynesians. Many, however, settled in the great Southeast Asian archipelago, forming communities of farmers, hunters and fishermen. Only on and around the island of New Guinea, where domestication of the root crop taro had enabled the Melanesians to create more complex settled societies, was the flood tide of Austronesian settlement broken. The eastern part of the archipelago remains a region of diminished Austronesian cultural and ethnic influence.[2]

The ecology of the islands had a profound influence on the nature of the societies which the Austronesian settlers created. In the interior of old, stable islands such as Kalimantan, the fragile rainforest ecology demanded a system of slash-and-burn agriculture, in which an area of forest was cleared and burnt, cultivated for a few years and then abandoned to lie fallow while the forest renewed itself over two decades or more. On islands such as Java, by contrast, where recent volcanic eruptions had created much of the landscape and given it great fertility, the Austronesians hacked expanding permanent settlements out of the jungle-covered volcanic slopes and directed abundant flowing water into irrigated rice fields. In the lowland swamps which fringe many of the islands, fishing became the source of livelihood, while in the dry limestone regions of the southeastern chain of islands,

2. Bellwood P. 1985 *Prehistory of the Indo-Malaysian Archipelago* (Academic Press, Sydney).

2

called Nusa Tenggara, the newcomers eked out a precarious existence from hardy rain-fed crops.

From about the first century AD a new source of diversity was imposed on this already complex world. A trade route linking the archipelago to India and China began to emerge, carrying not just the sophisticated manufactures of those great civilisations but also natural produce from the archipelago itself. Spices such as cloves and nutmeg, jungle products like camphor and dragon's blood, and exotic animal products from rhinoceros horns and bird-of-paradise pelts to beeswax and porcupine quills flowed from the archipelago to the ports of India and China. The new trade route created new economic opportunities as exports suddenly enlivened hitherto isolated communities. The narrow waters of the Strait of Melaka (Malacca), moreover, a key choke-point on the maritime trade route, soon supported a series of thriving communities, whose people we can now call Malays,[3] which not only traded produce from the interior but serviced merchants from elsewhere. Over the next twenty centuries, this trade route passed through periods of prosperity and decline, but it was always sufficiently important to form a counterbalance to the agricultural wealth of Java.

Malay traders, ranging north and west to China and India, brought back to their communities new wealth, new technologies and new ideas. Local chiefs, grown rich and powerful on trade, adopted Indian ideas of kingship, which exalted the monarch far above any status which had been possible in the early, somewhat egalitarian Austronesian communities. As a result, from about AD 300 the western islands of the archipelago came to be dotted with Hindu and Buddhist courts. From the fourth century to the fourteenth, Indian ideas of royal glory were at the heart of a series of empires in the archipelago based especially on either the agricultural wealth of Java or the trading profits of the Melaka Strait. Each power centre enjoyed times of pre-eminence, and raids between Sumatra and Java were frequent, but the two islands were never united in a single lasting polity. Division was a fact of political life in the archipelago from the start.

---

3. The term Malay can be used to distinguish the Austronesian inhabitants of the Indonesian archipelago from other Austronesians and, of course, other groups such as the Melanesians. It also, confusingly, refers to a major ethnic group from the coasts of Sumatra and the Malay peninsula, and to their language, which became the basis of modern Indonesian.

Distance from India and the political motives for conversion meant that the region was rather selective in its adoption of Indian religion: for instance, the four great classes of Hinduism – brahman, ksatriya, vaisya and sudra – were partly accepted, but not the multitude of smaller occupational castes. Indian religious ideas, however, gradually and unevenly seeped down from courts to communities, merging with the existing animist beliefs of the people and leaving a heritage of assumptions about royal authority and the lowly place of subjects, especially in Java and Bali, which peoples further east never experienced.

This cultural division was compounded by the later spread of Islam in the archipelago. Islam travelled with the trade routes, taking firm root during and after the thirteenth century and acquiring followers by virtue of the power of its message and because its egalitarian philosophy and system of commercial law was appealing to traders and to rulers who wished to attract trade to their ports. Muslim city states sprang up from Aceh to the spice islands of Maluku, sustaining a rich Muslim culture in touch with thought in the rest of the Muslim world. The existing Indian-influenced culture of the western archipelago at first blended easily with Islam, which had in any case passed through the softening influences of Persia and India before it arrived in the region. Thus rajas took the title of sultan but kept their authority as god-like rulers; peasants in the Javanese countryside paid respect to Allah but did not forget the old gods and spirits of the landscape. And not all regions were converted: Islam failed to penetrate much of the isolated interior of the larger islands, while the island of Bali, although involved in the trade routes which brought Islam, clung determinedly to its Hinduism. Christianity, carried to the archipelago as Catholicism by the Portuguese in the sixteenth century and as Protestantism by the Dutch in the seventeenth, simply increased the complexity, seeking converts amongst both non-Islamic and partially Islamised peoples, and benefiting from its association with Western technology and learning.

Only in the eighteenth century did stricter interpretations of Islam take firmer root in the region. The autocratic power of sultans was challenged by Islamic scholars and teachers (*ulama* and *kyai*) who asserted the primacy of religious doctrine and urged that local cultures be purged of pre-Islamic elements, from reverence for local spirits to female rule. This process, which continues today, took place unevenly. Aceh came under the dominance of stricter Muslims in the early eighteenth century, while the Minangkabau region immediately to the south underwent the same process a century later. In parts of Nusa Tenggara it began only in the twentieth century. On Java, this stricter interpretation of Islam took strongest root in the coastal regions, leaving the interior, especially in Central and East Java, dominated by an Islam which had intimately blended Islamic doctrine with Hindu and animist elements to create a distinctive belief system called *Kejawen*. The result, thus, was a patchwork of religious affiliation throughout the archipelago, with Muslims of widely varying degree alongside non-Muslims of many faiths.

COLONIALISM AND NATIONALISM

Political unity came to these disparate societies as a result of Dutch colonial expansion, but Dutch rule itself was a cause of further diversity. The Dutch seized control of the archipelago only gradually, taking regions one by one as it suited their economic and strategic interests. The spice islands of Maluku and the northwestern coast of Java came into Dutch hands in the early seventeenth century, with the rest of Java being annexed in the eighteenth century and much of Sumatra in the nineteenth. Some of the islands in Nusa Tenggara and parts of the interior of Sulawesi, Kalimantan and New Guinea did not come under effective Dutch control until the twentieth century. By the early twentieth century, full Dutch sovereignty had been established over a vast sweep of islands from Sumatra to New Guinea, but the boundaries of the Dutch domain were the somewhat arbitrary result of colonial negotiations with Britain, Spain, America, Portugal and Australia, and often ignored the ethnic and social character of the peoples whose allegiances were being decided. The almost-straight line which divided Dutch New Guinea from the German and British (later Australian) parts of the island separated Papuan tribes who, although they expended a good deal of energy in fighting each other, at least had more in common than they had with, say, the urbane Muslim merchants of the north Java coast. The border, too, which came to divide British Malaya from Dutch Sumatra divided a region which had formed a single cultural and economic unit for two millennia. The strongly Muslim regions of Sulu and Mindanao were left within the predominantly Catholic Philippines, while little but administrative convenience justified the division of Timor into Portuguese and Dutch zones.

The impact of colonial rule on different societies varied greatly. The people of the tiny Banda islands in Maluku were exterminated in the seventeenth century because they refused to accept a Dutch monopoly over nutmeg. In the same era, on the other hand, the clove-growing Minahasans of northern Sulawesi allied themselves with the Dutch East Indies Company and enthusiastically adopted Western religion and culture. Dutch trading restrictions stifled the prosperity of the Muslim city states of the north Java coast in the seventeenth and eighteenth centuries, but a congenial accommodation with colonial mining and plantation interests in the nineteenth century left the sultans in East Sumatra and East Kalimantan amongst the wealthiest men in the colony. The densely populated island of Java was the scene of brutal exploitation of peasant farmers, forced to grow crops for the colonial government, yet it also saw a growth in economic opportunities and, in the twentieth century, some of the earliest coherent development programmes in the world.

The Dutch also presided over a bewilderingly complex legal order in the Indies. Reluctant to treat their local subjects on the same footing as Dutch citizens, they installed a form of legal apartheid based first on religion and later on race, in which Europeans, so-called 'Foreign Orientals' (Chinese, Arabs and other non-Malays) and 'natives' were subject to separate forms of justice and different civil and political rights. They also preserved around 280 indirectly-ruled native states, where indigenous rulers played a greater role in day-to-day administration, as long as they closely followed the instructions of Dutch official Residents.

Dutch rule, however, did three things which helped to make Indonesia a possibility. First, the Dutch largely removed the possibility that any of the pre-colonial political units might pass unscathed through colonialism into a new independence. Dutch monopoly practices crippled the trading states of northern Java, making it unlikely that any of them might re-emerge as major independent identities. Dutch willingness to allow the British in Singapore and Penang to dominate the trade through the Melaka Strait did the same for the Malay states on the Sumatra coast. Determined Dutch military action against powerful kingdoms such as Makasar and Aceh shattered the economic base and strained the social cohesion of those societies, while elsewhere the co-option of indigenous rulers as clients of the colonial state created in them habits of dependence and deference which left them politically, militarily and financially unfit for life without Dutch backing.

Second, the Dutch chose to rule their Southeast Asian possessions as a single colony. The legal distinctions between races and between directly and indirectly ruled territories were subordinate to the colonial status of the Netherlands Indies as a whole. The governor-general in Batavia (now Jakarta) was the sole formal point of contact between the Indies and the metropolitan government, and the archipelago did not fracture like, say, the British territories in the Caribbean into a multitude of administrations separately responsible to the mother country. This meant that, for all its legal complexity, the Netherlands Indies evolved as a single state apparatus. Administrative measures were felt from one end of the archipelago to the other, officials were posted widely from region to region, and increasingly the indigenous peoples of the archipelago themselves began seeking their livelihoods within the new political framework, whether it was as contract labourers in the plantations of East Sumatra, as minor government officials or as students in the small number of elite educational institutions on Java. This administrative unity became especially important with the massive growth of government which took place from the late nineteenth century. As the colonial endeavour became more and more complex, technical expertise and administrative efficiency became increasingly indispensable and a vast governmental apparatus began to take shape. Departments of irrigation and transport, of trade and industry, of education and religion, began to grow and to intervene in the fabric of life in the colony, forming a powerful set of state institutions and strengthening the feeling amongst non-Europeans in the colony that control of the governor-general's palace in Batavia was the key to mastery of their affairs.

And third, the Dutch created a sense of grievance against their rule which led large numbers of Indonesians to conclude that the removal of colonial rule would be the single most effective means of solving their problems. Resentment of Dutch rule had many facets. In regions such as Aceh, where colonial rule had been imposed recently and in a welter of blood, an enduring bitterness poisoned relations between the colonialists and their subjects. Where Dutch economic interests had been strong, as in Java or the plantation region of East Sumatra, resentment focused on the enormous discrepancies in wealth and privilege between Europeans and natives. The debate over the precise economic consequences of colonial economic policies for the indigenous people of Java is complex and still unresolved[4] but abundant evidence certainly existed of impoverishment as a consequence of Dutch policy. Even where colonial rule had brought tangible benefits in the form of improved facilities, resentment festered as a result of colonial high-handedness in administration. Dutch measures to combat a serious outbreak of bubonic plague which occurred in the early twentieth century, for instance, although conducted with the welfare of the people at heart and using the most advanced techniques available, were deeply resented when they involved the destruction of rat-infested houses and when medical examination of victims included puncturing the spleen of victims' corpses, mutilation of the dead for any reason at all being anathema to Muslims.[5]

Racial discrimination, however, was perhaps the greatest source of resentment in the colony. As the administration of the colony became more sophisticated and complex, increasing numbers of indigenous people joined the cadre of colonial officials. An expanding education system took bright young men and turned them into physicians, engineers, clerks, lawyers and economists, and the colonial bureaucracy, once the exclusive preserve of Europeans, opened its lower doors to them. A quarter of a million natives were working in the colonial civil service by 1928, making up 90 per cent of the total staff. Although they generally served only in the lower levels of the colonial bureaucracy, their experience of education and their access to some of the levers of power gave them at least a degree of elite status. The more experienced they became, however, the more they chafed under the conventions of colonial discrimination which reserved senior posts, and the most generous salaries, for Europeans and preserved a petty social hierarchy under which natives were barred from fashionable clubs and swimming pools.

4. Two celebrated critiques of Dutch policies are worth mentioning here. Multatuli's semi-autobiographical novel, *Max Havelaar* (published in 1860), condemned the colonial authorities' alleged disregard for the welfare of their subjects in emotional terms, while Clifford Geertz (1963 *Agricultural Involution*. University of California Press, Berkeley) presented a complex argument which blamed what he saw as the stagnation and 'involution' of Javanese rural society on colonial policies. Geertz's arguments have set much of the agenda for the historical study of rural Java for three decades. An extensive critique and summary of the literature can be found in White B. 1983 'Agricultural Involution' and its critics: twenty years after. *Bulletin of Concerned Asian Scholars* 15(2): 18–31.

5. Hull T H 1987 *Plague in Java*. In Owen N (ed.) *Death and Disease in Southeast Asia. Explorations in Social, Medical and Demographic History* (Oxford University Press for the Asian Studies Association of Australia, Singapore), p. 212.

The movement to end Dutch rule which began to emerge in the early years of the twentieth century, therefore, drew from many sources, elite and mass, Christian and Muslim, Javanese and Acehnese. Most of its followers agreed to seek independence as a single country, and in 1928 the second national youth congress formally adopted an independent Indonesia as the nationalist goal[6] and ratified what became the national language, flag and anthem. This commitment to unity had two main roots. First, most opponents of the Dutch recognised the weakness of divided action. The Dutch had imposed their rule by tackling indigenous adversaries one by one, and in the early twentieth century they enjoyed enormous advantages in technology and organisation. Only by united action, the nationalists concluded, could the independence movement hope to prevail. Second, many of the leaders of the nationalist movement came from the new elite which had grown as a result of education and employment opportunities within the Netherlands Indies. Aspiring to the positions of authority held by the colonial establishment, few members of this elite favoured limiting their own future prospects by allowing the colony to fall into a number of smaller, separate states. The prospect of partition was even less attractive because so few of the old kingdoms and sultanates of the archipelago were politically or administratively viable and because restoring them would have given greater power to aristocratic and princely forces from the old order. To ensure that the fundamentals of politics were dictated by the modern elite, the unity of the Netherlands Indies had to be preserved after independence.

The Indonesian nationalist movement, therefore, embodied a paradox: although divided by enormous cultural, social and ideological differences it was permeated by an enthusiasm for national unity. This emphasis on unity concealed a wide variety of opinion on what form independent Indonesia should take. There were, first of all, those who regarded colonialism as a kind of gruelling apprenticeship to modernity. While deploring the brutalities, exploitation and discrimination of colonial rule, they nonetheless saw the West as having grasped universal human

---

6. The name Indonesia was, of course, not of local origin; in fact it was coined in Europe in 1850 as an anthropological term analogous to Polynesia and Melanesia. Nationalists seeking a suitable alternative to the term Netherlands Indies began to use it in the early twentieth century, and it soon became the generally accepted term amongst Indonesians, although the Dutch resisted using it officially until 1948.

values of freedom and justice, and they envisaged a modern Indonesian society based on principles of modernity and tolerance. A number of Indonesia's early leaders, including Muhammad Hatta and Sutan Sjahrir, belonged to this group. Educated in the Netherlands – Hatta in economics at Rotterdam and Sjahrir in law at Amsterdam – these men had seen a side of Dutch political culture and civilisation not easily visible to those who had experienced the Dutch mainly as colonial masters. This stream of thinking was ferocious in its denunciation of what it saw as the hypocrisies of colonial rule. When in 1915 the Dutch in the Indies prepared to celebrate the centenary of their liberation from Napoleonic rule, Suwardi Suryaningrat responded scathingly: 'If I were a Dutchman, I would not organise an independence celebration in a country where the independence of the people has been stolen.'[7] These modernising nationalists found a good deal of encouragement amongst progressive circles in the colonial establishment, who looked towards a future partnership between the Dutch and the indigenous peoples of the archipelago, based on Western education and efficient administration, but they generally parted company with Dutch progressives over how soon independence should come: even the most radical amongst the Dutch generally argued for a lengthy period of preparation for independence, while the nationalists maintained that waiting simply prolonged dependence and that independence itself was the only proper training for self-reliance.

In contrast to the modernising nationalists, Indonesia's communists took a far less enthusiastic view of colonialism, regarding its injustices as fundamental to the capitalist system. With no more than a tiny local industrial working class, they could not argue the then orthodox line which gave revolutionary primacy to the industrial proletariat. Instead, they argued that all Indonesians had become proletarians as a result of their subordination to international capitalism, and that the only remedy was the elimination of foreign capital. Marxism was a powerful ideological force partly because it presented the Indonesian people unambiguously as victims of colonialism, rather than partially as beneficiaries. It proposed that Indonesians themselves should take their future into their hands and make a revolution against the Dutch, and

7. Suwardi S 1913 Als ik eens Nederlander was. Cited in Anderson B R O'G 1983 *Imagined Communities. Reflections on the Origin and Spread of Nationalism* (Verso, London), p. 108.

it lined up the class struggle with the national struggle, giving all Indonesians a place on the side of the proletarian struggle against capitalism and colonialism.

Islam, for its part, also presented a powerful critique of colonialism. Formal Islamic doctrine largely prohibits Muslims from accepting non-Muslim rule and to many Muslims the colonial order was a deep religious affront, even though in the early twentieth century the colonial authorities adopted a policy of giving financial support to Islamic religious institutions. Islam also took exception to social injustice, especially to the use of debt and interest charges as a technique for trapping peasants and labourers in permanent obligation to colonial capitalists.

And finally, there was a neo-traditionalist stream of thought, generally the least articulate of the four, which saw the key to national resurgence in a revitalisation of the older traditions of the archipelago. Although this stream encompassed a small number of ambitious petty sultans and rajas, it was most strongly represented amongst the traditional elite of Java, called the *priyayi*. After the constriction or elimination of Java's former independent sultanates, these aristocratic administrators had shifted their allegiance to the Dutch, becoming the principal Javanese agents of colonial rule. The Dutch in turn encouraged them to present themselves to their subjects as minor sovereigns, complete with court and ceremonial regalia. They looked back on early Javanese kingdoms such as fourteenth century Majapahit and hoped that with the departure of colonialism, something of this early glory and prosperity could be recreated.

Each of these ideological streams, however, left major political issues unresolved. In taking the view, for instance, that Dutch stubbornness was the main obstacle to Indonesian prosperity, the modernising nationalists did not confront difficult questions such as the place of foreign economic interests, especially in the plantation sector, in independent Indonesia. The communists, while seeing all Indonesian social groups as part of a broad proletariat, were generally silent on the kind of internal social reforms they might demand if they were in power. The Islamic critique of colonialism left unresolved the extent to which Islamic law might be imposed on non-Muslim minorities and on unwilling Muslims, and was ambiguous on what kinds of capitalist activity should be tolerated. And the neo-traditionalist stream, of course, left unresolved the difficult question of which aspects of fourteenth-century Java might be inappropriate for the twentieth century.

11

Although it is possible in retrospect to speak of separate streams of ideological thought in the Indonesian nationalist movement, the picture during the Dutch colonial era itself was never clear-cut, with most nationalists drawing in some degree from two or more streams to create a critique of colonialism and then to gather a coalition to oppose it. In the second decade of the twentieth century, an Islamic–communist movement was influential, arguing that the Prophet Muhammad had been the first socialist. From the late 1920s, the most dynamic political thinker in the colony was Sukarno.[8] Unlike Hatta and Sjahrir, he had not studied in Europe, and his ideology evolved into an eclectic blend of all the major streams of thought in the emerging Indonesian movement. All of the nationalist thinkers, however, lacked the means to make their intentions a reality by removing the Dutch. In the twentieth century, the Dutch had long since ceased to be a world power. They retained, nevertheless, a sizeable and flexible colonial army, well-armed and experienced in counter-insurgency warfare; they maintained an efficient political police which, although it was known for neither brutality nor arbitrary arrest, maintained a network of informers and agents which kept a close watch on dissidents; and they enjoyed the prestige of European power and the image of European invincibility which came with Europe's domination of the world since the mid nineteenth century.

Against colonial power, the nationalists attempted a variety of strategies. Early in the second decade of the twentieth century, a Muslim mass organisation called Sarekat Islam presented the first concerted demand for independence, but crumbled after the colonial authorities disregarded its claim. In 1926–27, the communist party (PKI) staged a small string of abortive armed uprisings against colonial rule which were suppressed with contemptuous ease by the authorities, who exiled surviving party members to the jungles of West New Guinea. During the late 1920s and early 1930s Sukarno attempted to summon together an irresistible coalition to demand independence, but this attempt was likewise stymied by his arrest and exile, while an ambitious long-term plan by Hatta and Sjahrir to train a nationalist cadre before confronting the Dutch was also ended by Dutch police action. For the rest of the 1930s, nationalists were reduced to attempting – mostly without success – to argue concessions out of the Dutch in the semi-representative People's Council or Volksraad.

8. Many Indonesians, especially those from Java, have only one name.

When the colonial era finally came to an end with the Japanese invasion in 1942, the nationalist movement was deeply committed to the principle of Indonesian unity. It had not, however, resolved just what content that unity should possess. On fundamental issues, ranging from the form of government and the relationship of the individual to the state to the place of religion in government policy and the legitimacy of regional ethnicities, there was no consensus. Nor was there a political force which appeared likely to be able to impose its vision of independent Indonesia on the rest of society. The PKI, schooled by years of repression, had probably the greatest resilience of any political organisation; of all the nationalist leaders Sukarno had perhaps the widest following and Muslim political groups were perhaps the most closely enmeshed with peasant society, at least in some regions. But none of these political interests had the popular support and organisational strength to turn itself into the pre-eminent political force in the country, let alone to displace the apparently immovable colonial authorities. If one had attempted in, say, 1935 to predict the future of the Netherlands Indies, one might have forecast that the *priyayi* of Java, along with the multi-ethnic technical bureaucracy of the colonial state, would be the eventual beneficiaries of a gradual Dutch handover of power. Even at this stage, however, some far-sighted Indonesians had begun to hope that rising Japanese military strength in Asia might break through the log-jam of Dutch colonial power. That hope became reality with the outbreak of the Second World War in Asia.

JAPANESE OCCUPATION

During a little over three years of occupation from 1942 to 1945, Japan's destruction of Dutch power was thorough. The colonial army, defeated in a humiliatingly brief campaign, was consigned to detention camps. Indonesian soldiers were soon released, but for the rest of the war the Europeans remained behind barbed wire where European civilians joined them as soon as Japanese replacements for senior and technical positions could be found. Many posts vacated by the Dutch went temporarily or permanently to Indonesians, giving them greater experience of administrative power. The use of Dutch was banned and European superiority was systematically demolished by measures such as forcing Europeans to perform menial tasks in public. The colonial economy, too, was reoriented to the needs of Japan. Crops such as tea and sugar, which no longer had access to their former markets, were scrapped in favour of food production and crops useful to the war effort such as rami and castor. In the absence of spare parts from the outside world, the once-smooth machinery of colonial production gradually began to seize up, to rust, to wear out and to fail, unless it could be turned to the war effort and kept alive by the cannibalisation of other machinery. This destruction, part deliberate, part simply neglectful, ensured that the Netherlands Indies of pre-war times could never be restored.

The Japanese occupation also deeply wounded the old colonial bureaucracy, which had been the Indonesian group closest to power in the old order. Although the bureaucracy benefited from promotion to posts vacated by the Dutch, the Japanese employed it to administer many of the more oppressive aspects of their rule, such as the recruitment of forced labour and the requisition of rice supplies. Both policies caused enormous hardship: tens of thousands of Indonesian labourers, receiving minimal pay and suffering meagre nutrition, brutal treatment and appalling health conditions, worked for the Japanese on military and economic projects which often turned out to be misguided or pointless. The collection of rice for redistribution to the occupation forces and the general population was so ineptly handled that thousands of tonnes rotted in stores or were eaten by rats while people starved. The bureaucracy could hardly avoid being associated with other unpleasant aspects of the occupation, too, such as a critical shortage of consumer items, as a result of the wartime shortage of raw materials, factory capacity and shipping space in Japan's Asian empire. It was under these circumstances, moreover, that Indonesia's bureaucracy learnt enduring habits of corruption, made possible by the tangle of Japanese wartime regulations and necessary by the steadily declining standard of living in Indonesia. The calm, efficient administrative corps of the colonial era comprehensively disqualified itself from political leadership in the three years of the occupation.

Even though the Japanese removed the main opponent of the nationalists, Indonesian independence might still not have been achieved had the Japanese not sponsored movement towards a quasi-independent puppet state in the former Dutch colony. One of Japan's principal political strategies in its occupied territories was to create nominally independent states in which Japanese garrison commanders and ambassadors could continue to demand

14

particular policies and programmes, while the Japanese themselves were freed of the distractions of day-to-day administration and somewhat insulated from popular resentment of their policies. The Japanese were relatively late to move towards puppet rule in Indonesia, partly because Indonesia's oil-fields were so important a resource that the naval authorities in particular were unwilling to give them up, partly because many Japanese policy-makers hoped during the early part of the war that an intensive programme of cultural Japanisation might make the Indonesians positively enthusiastic about Japanese rule.

As the war turned in favour of the Allies, however, shipments of oil and other products to Japan were cut off and the obstacles to imbuing Japanese values quickly became clear; the Japanese authorities then began a somewhat hasty programme to prepare Indonesia for the puppet independence which they had already granted to Burma and the Philippines. With the Japanese forces in steady retreat, the Japanese may have hoped that a newly independent Indonesia would hamper the Allied advance. This was probably one of their motives in setting up an Indonesian auxiliary army – called the PETA in Java and the Giyugun in Sumatra – in October 1943. To lead the independence process, they selected Sukarno and Hatta, prominent nationalists whom they had already used for general propaganda purposes and whose antagonism to the Dutch had led them to look on the Japanese as a necessary, temporary evil. The two men led a headlong rush for independence from May 1945, hoping to hold independence in their hands before the expected Allied victory.

Even under these urgent circumstances, however, the sheer vagueness of the idea of Indonesia became apparent. Debates in the Preparatory Committee for Indonesian Independence (Panitia Persiapan Kemerdekaan Indonesia: PPKI) on the basis of the state led to stalemate over the desirable constitutional position of Islam. Eventually, in what became known as the Jakarta Charter, the nationalists agreed that Indonesia should not be an Islamic state, but that its Muslim citizens should be obliged to follow Islamic law, though by some sleight of hand this clause was omitted from the final version of the constitution. Sukarno made a major contribution to smoothing over differences by proposing as the basis of the state a set of five principles which he called the Pancasila and which, he said, were shared by all Indonesians, regardless of their ethnicity or political beliefs. These principles, enshrined in the preamble to the new constitution, were as follows:

Belief in God
National Unity
Humanitarianism
People's Sovereignty
Social Justice and Prosperity.

As a guide to policy and politics, of course, these principles needed amplification. As before, however, the need to secure independence overshadowed the task of defining its content. When independence day was set for late August, the final consummation of nationalist hopes seemed at last to be imminent. The atomic bombs, however, fell on Hiroshima and Nagasaki, and Japan surrendered on 15 August 1945.

Nationalist disappointment and frustration was tempered by two considerations. First, Japanese-sponsored independence granted on the eve of Japan's defeat was hardly likely to count for much in international affairs, and in any case independence as a gift was less desirable than independence seized by the Indonesian people themselves. And second, and more important, at the time of the surrender the victorious Allied forces were still far away from Java and other centres of power in Indonesia. Indonesian nationalists were suddenly left with what seemed like a golden opportunity to take their future into their own hands and to declare an independence that was by grace of neither Japanese nor Dutch. After intense discussion in the forty-eight hours following the surrender, Sukarno and Hatta agreed to declare independence in a brief ceremony in Sukarno's garden in Jakarta on the morning of 17 August 1945.

Indonesia now existed as an independent state, at least in the minds of those present at the ceremony. But it had come into existence with basic questions of national identity and political form still unresolved and with its own survival very much in question. The following years were to be occupied with resolving these issues.

CHAPTER TWO

Independence Undefined, 1945–49

Indonesia struggled with the Netherlands for over four years before the Dutch finally recognised its independence. During this time, the Dutch reconquered large tracts of the country in an intermittent series of campaigns between longer periods of fractious negotiation and uneasy ceasefire. Eventually they gave up in the face of growing international pressure and an increasingly unmanageable guerrilla resistance in the archipelago. No one has even attempted to calculate the human toll of Indonesia's war of independence, but certainly tens of thousands, possibly over a hundred thousand Indonesians, died in defending the new Republic against the returning colonial power.

The years of warfare and negotiation fundamentally shaped the character of independent Indonesian politics. They gave Indonesian nationalists, first, an enduring pride which at least partly wiped out the humiliation of Dutch repression and collaboration with the Japanese. Popular involvement in the resistance, moreover, firmly established the principle of mass political participation which underpinned politics for the next two decades. The outcome of the conflict also left a clear message that dogged struggle in the face of formidable odds could lead to victory, a lesson Indonesian political forces were to apply to their domestic struggle for power after independence was secured. But the war of independence also left a legacy of political bitterness within what was once, for all its divisions, a single nationalist movement, reshaping the alignment of political forces and creating deep fractures between former political allies and associates. The struggle also left many things unresolved. Certainly the prime political goal of the Republic's leaders, internationally recognised independence, had been achieved. But the domestic politics of the state were far less clearly resolved, largely because of the state's continuing weakness in the face of the social and political forces which the Japanese surrender and the independence proclamation unleashed. Neither the ideological character of the state nor the status of its various minorities was decided. The Republic which began its struggle with one provisional constitution in August 1945 ended its war of independence in December 1949 with another.

THE STRUGGLE WITH THE DUTCH

In creating an Indonesian state out of a Dutch colony, the leaders of the Republic faced two distinct tasks: they had to achieve international recognition for the independence of the state they were creating, and they had to deliver to their people the fruits of independence, in the form of policies to tackle the problems left by colonialism. Without international recognition, the Republic would languish on the margins of international politics, constantly vulnerable to Dutch efforts to regain colonial control; without taking at least the first steps towards reshaping society, the Republic would have little basis on which to demand the loyalty of its citizens. The two tasks, however, were often contradictory. To satisfy the demands of the international community, the Republic had to emphasise continuity with the colonial order in precisely those areas, such as economic and social policy, where the nationalist demand for action was strongest. Faced with this contradiction, successive Republican governments invariably gave priority to the goal of international recognition, even though this frequently put them in conflict with domestic political opinion.

Although we now appreciate that Western colonialism was in the process of disappearing from Southeast Asia, the Indonesian Republic seemed at the time to be facing formidable odds. The main immediate cause for concern on the part of the Republic's leaders was the Japanese, who were still in control of most of Java and Sumatra. During the war many senior occupation officials had supported the nationalists, and they had carried Sukarno and Hatta to the brink of independence. After the surrender, however, they shrank from recognising the new state, because the terms of their surrender to the Allies obliged them to maintain the political status quo in their occupied territories pending the arrival of British and Dutch forces.

Thus Republican leaders moved cautiously to assert their authority, avoiding any actions which might provoke the Japanese into crushing their initiative on the spot. The Central Indonesian National Committee or KNIP, the country's quasi-parliament, adopted a provisional constitution and elected Sukarno and Hatta president and vice-president of the Republic respectively. Sukarno appointed the Republic's first cabinet at the end of August. The ministers named in that cabinet set about the task of establishing a functioning bureaucracy loyal to the Republic and fairly quickly attracted the support of most of the Indonesians who had previously served the Dutch colonial and Japanese occupation bureaucracies.[1] And steps were taken towards the establishment of a Republican army, though these steps were tentative and even the use of the term 'army' (*tentara*) was avoided until October.

Many of the institutions being set up by the Republican government, however, existed more in the minds of their creators than in the reality of Indonesian political life. The Republican leadership, for all its apparatus of government, had virtually no territory under its control. The independence of the Republic was unrecognised internationally and a shadow of counter-attack hung over the new government, paralysing decision-making. Not only was there a risk that the Japanese would intervene to restore the political status quo but it was only a matter of time before Allied forces, including Dutch units, would land in the main cities to commence the task of re-establishing colonial authority. The task of preserving the Republic's existence overshadowed the need to carry out any of the nationalist programmes.

The Republic's leaders, therefore, began to petition the Allies for recognition, mounting plausible but ineffective arguments that the rapid Dutch surrender in 1942 had extinguished Dutch sovereignty and maintaining forcefully that the Republic of 17 August 1945 was not the puppet state which the Japanese had intended to declare a few days later. In order to reinforce this position, the new Republic's presidential constitution was quietly shelved and in mid November Sutan Sjahrir, the most prominent of the small group of nationalist leaders who had refused to cooperate with the Japanese, was installed as executive prime minister. Sukarno, still president, was shunted into more ceremonial duties, while Hatta as vice-president exercised his

1. Cf. Kahin G McT 1972 *Nationalism and Revolution in Indonesia* (1st Cornell Paperbacks edn, Cornell University Press, Ithaca), p. 139.

formidable influence over government policy informally. Under Sjahrir's leadership, the Republic also presented itself as being no threat to Western economic interests in the Indies. The Republic, Sjahrir told the world, would insist on remedying the injustices of the colonial order, but would not seek to take Indonesia out of the Western capitalist bloc.

This arrangement in many ways suited the personalities of all three men. Sukarno was a visionary and an orator, a man whose words could hold Indonesian audiences spellbound for hours at a time as he conjured up images of a glorious past, a challenging present and a glittering future. When speaking to intellectuals, he offered dazzling verbal fireworks, mixing concepts from Western philosophers with aphorisms drawn from indigenous tradition; speaking to the poor, he tapped powerful folk myths and earthy peasant common sense. He was tall, handsome and somewhat vain, with a reputation as a seducer of women. Although his energy was impressive, he tired quickly of administrative detail and was happiest in the roles of reconciling political opponents and of receiving honour. Hatta, on the other hand, was a rather dour and unprepossessing Minangkabau from West Sumatra, owing his political position to the sheer force of his intellect. He had little public presence, but was a consummate planner, at his best when working out practicalities behind the scenes. Sjahrir, a close colleague of Hatta from the early years of the nationalist movement, was a much more demonstrative politician than his fellow Minangkabau. During the Japanese occupation, he had cultivated links with a salon of young intellectuals in Jakarta, who gave him a better insight into the mood of the revolutionary youth in 1945 than either Sukarno or Hatta. With an incisive mind, a sharp tongue and a brittle ego, Sjahrir had no real popular touch, but his energy, intellect and commitment to modernity made him the ideal person to attempt to persuade the Western world that Indonesia could and should run its own affairs.

The caution of these men was not shared by ordinary Indonesians, however, who greeted the Republic with an enormous outpouring of enthusiasm. As news of the independence proclamation spread through the archipelago, local national committees sprang up to coordinate the transition to independence, hoisting the national flag and announcing their readiness to accept instructions from the national government in Jakarta. Few instructions came. Even when reliable communications became possible between Jakarta and outlying regions, the Republican leadership was reluctant to do anything which might have upset the political balance.

Within a few weeks of the independence declaration, however, the Republic's supporters were in at least nominal control of much of the country, having cajoled or intimidated some Japanese forces to hand over their weapons. Nonetheless, the Republic was unable to prevent seasoned Allied troops – British Indian forces in Java and Sumatra, Australians in the east – from landing in the main cities.[2] In some places the Allies landed unopposed but in others Indonesians resisted fiercely. The heaviest fighting was in the East Java capital of Surabaya in November 1945, where Indonesians fought a determined street battle against Allied troops who were supported by shelling from British warships in Surabaya harbour. Even there, however, the Indonesians were forced to give way.[3]

The battle of Surabaya convinced the British that to keep their troops in Indonesia would mean committing them to involvement in a protracted war to recover the countryside. This was politically intolerable both to public opinion in Britain and to the nationalist movement in India, a matter of considerable consequence given the numbers of Indian troops under British command in Indonesia. The British thus pressed both sides to negotiate towards an agreed independence programme; but they kept their armed forces in Indonesia long enough to allow the Dutch to assemble a military force of their own capable of resuming the task of conquest.

The Republic's leaders, too, drew lessons from their experience of the first few weeks of independence. They recognised that their earlier policy of accommodating the West had brought them no closer to foreign recognition, and that it had been the resistance to the British in Surabaya which had done most to win international support for their cause. The Republic moved accordingly into what was to be its strategy until the eventual achievement of Dutch acquiescence in independence. There were two elements to this strategy. On the one hand, the Republicans were prepared to negotiate with the Dutch, securing whatever concessions might be possible through such means while being prepared themselves to concede virtually anything which might later be recovered or

2. The first large-scale landings in Java by Allied troops – British and Indian – did not take place until 30 September, and then only in Jakarta. Semarang and Surabaya were not reoccupied until late October. In Sumatra, Medan and Padang were reoccupied in mid October.
3. See Frederick W H 1988 *Visions and Heat: The Making of the Indonesian Revolution* (Ohio University Press, Athens).

restored after independence. On the other hand, to back up this strategy they applied a combination of military and diplomatic pressure to the Dutch in the hope that they could be coerced into making concessions. From November 1945, accordingly, the Republic's government began turning its efforts to creating an Indonesian revolutionary army. The government rejected from the start the possibility that armed force alone could eject the Dutch, but depended on its armed forces to prevent the Dutch from simply overrunning the Republic. The Republic also sought foreign diplomatic support, partly by continuing the appeal on the basis of principles of self-determination, partly by arguing that colonial rule was now so unpalatable to Indonesians that the Dutch would never be able to restore the degree of peace and order necessary for the smooth functioning of Western enterprises.

The first armed units of the new Indonesian army had emerged from remnants of the Japanese-sponsored PETA and Giyugun, but most of these had few weapons at first and little battle experience. In attempting to turn this ramshackle force into a modern army, the civilian government found its greatest ally in Abdul Haris Nasution, a Sumatran who had undergone Dutch officer training on the eve of the Japanese invasion and who quickly emerged after the declaration of independence as commander of the new Siliwangi Division in West Java. Nasution combined a thorough understanding of military organisation with a strategic perceptiveness and a sensitivity to the complicated political and diplomatic position of the Republic's civilian leaders. His vision of a modern, Western-style army which could defeat the Dutch forces on their own terms fitted well with Sjahrir's strategy of negotiating from strength, and he might have been still more influential but for his aloof and sometimes dogmatic confidence in his own correctness, which tended to alienate potential allies.

The Indonesian–Dutch negotiations which dominated 1946 were a tortured affair, the two sides sometimes implacably opposed, sometimes seeming to be separated by no more than a thin margin of interpretation. Eventually, under British pressure, they reached a grudging agreement in the mountain resort of Linggajati in West Java and Sumatra) and two still-to-be-created federal states of become independent as a federation between the Republic (on Java and Sumatra) and two still to be created federal states of Borneo and eastern Indonesia. The discussions, however, and the Linggajati Agreement itself were essentially a sham: the aim of the Dutch was to persuade the Republic to accept some form of colonial sovereignty which would enable Dutch forces to purge the country of anti-colonial elements, while the Republic's negotiators were willing to make far-reaching concessions to the Dutch, knowing that once the Dutch had relinquished sovereignty then Indonesia as an independent state would be free to undertake whatever programme of economic, social or political reform it chose. The Linggajati Agreement, therefore, measured the depth of division between the two sides, rather than the extent of agreement, and the apparent rapport between the two antagonists soon disintegrated in a spate of accusations and counter-accusations, culminating in a Dutch invasion of the Republic in July 1947.

In this invasion – which for political reasons they preferred to call a 'police action' – the Dutch seized half the Republic's territory on Java as well as the richest areas on Sumatra but failed to make the nationalists more tractable. During the seventeen month ceasefire which followed, another treaty – the so-called *Renville* Agreement – was signed and broken, much like that of Linggajati, before the Dutch launched another attack in December 1948, designed to wipe the Republic off the face of the archipelago. The Dutch, however, had miscalculated. Since 1945, Indonesia had developed important contacts with India, Australia and other neighbouring countries, who now gave it valuable diplomatic support as its overseas representatives sought international condemnation of the Dutch. Moreover, although the Republic's provisional capital at Yogyakarta in central Java was captured, along with Sukarno, Hatta and most of the cabinet, guerrilla resistance in the countryside began to weigh down the Dutch military machine. Unable to deliver a quick victory, the Netherlands itself became vulnerable to fears in the United States that a protracted guerrilla war would open the way to communist revolution in Indonesia. Diplomatic pressure, including an American threat to withhold Marshall Plan aid from the Netherlands, induced the Dutch to crumble. They restored Sukarno and Hatta to Yogyakarta and began yet another round of negotiations at what was called the Round Table Conference, which led this time to a formal transfer of sovereignty to the Republic in the last days of 1949. Although other Asian nations – India, Burma, the Philippines – had been granted independence by this time, Vietnam was still in the midst of its apocalyptic struggle with the French and Indonesians could claim accordingly that they were the first in Asia to win independence in the teeth of armed resistance.

Pride in this achievement remains at the centre of Indonesian political awareness.

Defeat of the Dutch, however, was no more than a partial victory for Indonesian nationalism. By the terms of the independence agreement the nationalists had to accept a complicated constitutional structure under which the Republic of Indonesia, which they had declared as a sovereign state in 1945, became merely a constituent member of a federal Republic of the United States of Indonesia along with fifteen much smaller states created across the archipelago under Dutch auspices. This federal Republic in turn was part of a Netherlands–Indonesian Union under the Dutch crown. Even more serious, the Dutch retained de facto control of the western half of the island of New Guinea, previously regarded as an integral part of the Netherlands Indies and thus also of Indonesia. For many nationalists, therefore, the formal transfer of sovereignty in December 1949 was no more than a step on the road to full independence.

MASS POLITICS

An even greater legacy of the struggle was mass politics. The declaration of independence presented the Indonesian people with the new and powerful proposition that they were now masters of their own destiny. The Dutch had never hinted at a popular democratic path to independence, nor had this principle attracted much support in the pre-war nationalist movement: the ideal of Indonesian independence was generally represented as a coalition of ethnic and class groups, with elite leaders from each group assumed to be speaking on behalf of their respective communities. After August 1945, however, with the Republic too weak to impose its will on them, and its leaders distracted by the pressing needs of political survival, Indonesians proceeded to create a new independent order as they believed it should be.

This new order began with the settling of old scores. In a series of social revolutions across Java and Sumatra, Indonesian people took rough justice into their hands and attacked those they believed had upheld the oppression of the Dutch and Japanese regimes. Three groups were the main target of these social revolutions. In many regions, Indonesians who had worked for and with the colonial and occupation governments were swept from office. In Aceh, the chief victims were the feudal chiefs whose defection to the Dutch in the late nineteenth century had enabled colonial power to establish itself; in nearby East Sumatra, the main targets were the Malay sultans, who had grown immensely wealthy on the proceeds of the plantation sector. In many parts of Java, the old *priyayi* were toppled, sometimes killed, sometimes publicly humiliated, sometimes simply driven away. Second, the Chinese communities of Java and Sumatra were a major target, resented because of their relative privilege under colonialism, and because of their uncertain allegiance to the Republic, and plundered because of their wealth, though not all Chinese were wealthy. And third, the Europeans and Eurasians who emerged from the Japanese detention camps were bewildered to find themselves confronted by deep hatred and a haphazard campaign of terror and assassination directed against them by Indonesians who saw them as a vanguard of returning colonialism.

The sweeping away of the old order throughout much of the Republic left regional politics open to local forces with their own visions of what the Republic should be.[4] In Aceh, for instance, Muslim religious leaders took power and established something close to an Islamic administration; on the northern coast of Central Java, the local communist party briefly seized control of the administration and began a programme to place the local economy under centrally coordinated cooperatives. In the old court city of Yogyakarta, the progressive sultan, Hamengku Buwono IX, moved rapidly into leadership, forestalling a more radical outbreak, while in the countryside east of Jakarta, a powerful coalition of local gangsters seized power and began to subject their region to a blend of extortion and self-determination. Even where the consequences of local self-determination were less spectacular, the independence struggle quickly established a tradition of local political self-reliance. With the Republic's leaders unable to guarantee its security, people flocked into local armed organisations, generally based on existing social nuclei such as schools, community associations, boy scout troops, criminal bands and the like, with the aim of forming a bulwark against Allied invasion. Inevitably, many of these 'struggle organisations', as they were called, lined up with, or were even sponsored by, the political

4. On these social revolutions, see Kahin A R (ed.) 1985 *Regional Dynamics of the Indonesian Revolution: Unity from Diversity* (University of Hawaii Press, Honolulu). For a full discussion of the events in northern Sumatra, see Reid A J S 1979 *The Blood of the People: Revolution and the End of Traditional Rule in Northern Sumatra* (Oxford University Press, Kuala Lumpur).

parties which had began to emerge in November 1945. Local leaders were thus not only able to capture the spiritual leadership of the independence struggle but also to acquire the backing of armed force to support their political positions.

Paradoxically, the Republic's weakness at the outset was one of its greatest strengths: it alienated very few and encouraged all to believe that they had the power and the right to shape its character as they saw fit. Increasingly, however, it became clear to the Republic's leaders that defining the Republic had a role to play in their strategy for securing independence. And it became clear to the Indonesian public at large that the strategy adopted to secure independence would play an important role in beginning to define the Republic.

In late 1945 concern began to grow amongst many Indonesians that concessions to the West were committing the Republic to policies which were fundamentally opposed to the aspirations of the nationalist movement. The Sjahrir government argued that these concessions were unavoidable in the struggle to achieve international recognition. However, a radical nationalist group, focused on a former communist leader, Tan Malaka, emerged to argue that Sjahrir and his colleagues had underestimated the fighting will of the Indonesian people.[5] They argued that if the Republic undertook a radical programme of social and economic reform, especially including the elimination of Dutch interests and influences, then the Indonesian people's stake in independence would be so great that they would overcome all odds in its defence. The movement, called the Persatuan Perjuangan, or Struggle Union, assembled a wide coalition of forces, both idealists who saw in Sjahrir's concessions to the Dutch a fundamental betrayal of nationalist principles, and opportunists who saw a chance for their own power if Sjahrir could be toppled. In early 1946 it achieved enormous popularity, leaving Sjahrir so isolated that he felt compelled to resign as prime minister. His opponents, however, united enough to achieve his removal, were not united enough to replace him. As soon as the Tan Malaka group had achieved the popular goal of removing Sjahrir and seemed poised to move beyond the simple rejection of compromise with the Dutch and towards implementing its radical programme, the coalition which had once backed it began to crumble. The political process

5. On Tan Malaka and his movement, see Anderson B R O'G 1972 *Java in a Time of Revolution: Occupation and Resistance 1944–1946* (Cornell University Press, Ithaca).

was stalemated and Sukarno intervened to reappoint Sjahrir as prime minister. Sjahrir in turn exploited the divisions amongst his challengers to construct a somewhat broader government and he thus survived the challenge. Once reinstated, moreover, he had Tan Malaka arrested and detained without trial.

The Tan Malaka challenge was a pivotal event for the early Republic, for it demonstrated the disunity which existed within the nationalist movement on all but the most fundamental of issues, and because it marked the first occasion on which control of the Republican state played a key role in the outcome of a national political conflict. Sukarno's intervention from the presidency and Sjahrir's deployment of armed force to remove Tan Malaka from the scene were the first signs that the political forces which controlled the state would enjoy a powerful role in defining the nation.

STATE AUTHORITY

The contours of the Republican state during the independence struggle are difficult to map. On paper there existed a centralised hierarchy, proceeding from the president's temporary residence in Yogyakarta, through the cabinet and on through an orderly ranking of government departments and offices on the one hand and military units on the other. In practice, the authority of the central government was limited, conditional and widely fluctuating from region to region and time to time. The principles of self-determination and popular sovereignty were as powerful within government institutions as they were within society as a whole, and a great many government offices and armed units acquired their first independence-era heads by election. The Republican government, moreover, was critically short of money for much of the war and was seldom able to establish its authority by financial sanctions. Implementing government policies, therefore, and even determining military tactics and strategy, were generally a matter of careful negotiation and calculation of relative power positions. It was a fluid situation, dependent on changing personal alliances and shifting strategic imperatives.

The Republican government, however, put a high priority on tightening its authority in two areas. The first was over openly insubordinate local governments. Although willing to accept a high degree of local autonomy in practice, at least for the time being, the

Republic was not prepared to accept local administrations which formally cut themselves off from the Republic's authority. As soon as it had the ability, therefore, it moved to disband the local communist government on the northern coast of Central Java, along with similar smaller experiments in the vicinity of Jakarta and in West Sumatra.

The second area where the Republic especially emphasised its own authority was in the armed forces. Not only had most armed units elected their own leaders, sometimes accepting, sometimes rejecting the Japanese-trained PETA and Giyugun officers, but senior officers had assembled in November 1945 to elect their own army commander. Their choice, General Sudirman, was a man of uncomplicated patriotism and deep concern for the welfare of his subordinates who quickly captured the loyalty of large parts of the army. A former PETA officer, Sudirman drew about himself a like-minded group of officers who had acquired from the Japanese military a mistrust of civilian authority. This mistrust had been compounded by a feeling that the Republic had neglected its military strategy during the first weeks after the Japanese surrender, when the civilian leaders had concentrated on avoiding a Japanese crackdown. Contemptuous of Western military training and tactics, these officers rejected the idea that their forces might not be a match militarily for the Allied troops and they chafed under the truces and ceasefires which the negotiations with the Dutch called for from time to time. Amir Sjarifuddin, as Sjahrir's deputy and defence minister, played a key role in gradually edging Sudirman and his colleagues out of direct command positions and installing in their place a group of young, Dutch-trained officers, of whom Nasution and T.B. Simatupang were soon to become the most influential. The Sjarifuddin–Nasution alliance was also instrumental in channelling the Republic's limited resources into what were seen as the most reliable units, including Nasution's own Siliwangi Division in West Java. They also combined political and organisational resources to begin the long process of incorporating or suppressing the vast number of independent-minded armed units, inside and outside the army, which were scattered across the face of the country.

Although these measures brought about greater internal discipline in the army and greater obedience to the civilian authorities, the military hierarchy remained critically weak, with local units closely aligning themselves to rival political forces and the high command subjecting government instructions to suspicious inspection before deciding whether and how to act. The army's self-confidence as an independent political agent was strengthened by a growing myth of its own origins and role in the independence war, a myth of an army which virtually created itself, setting up its own institutions and depending for its logistical and financial support on its own efforts and on the direct backing of the Indonesian people. This legend had begun with the Sudirman's complaint that the new Republican government had not moved quickly enough to create an army in August 1945, and was reinforced by the difficult logistical and financial circumstances of the army for the entire war of independence. Although the armed forces always received the lion's share of the Republic's budget, that was never enough and army units were forced to supplement their incomes by direct arrangements with local traders and by direct contributions from the people. The myth became established as canon after the second Dutch attack of later 1948, when the civilian cabinet allowed itself to be captured by the Dutch and the armed forces were indeed the major force standing between the Republic and extinction. This practical autonomy and self-confidence, however, were to survive well beyond the independence struggle, making the struggle for dominance within the Indonesian armed forces a major sub-theme in the struggle for dominance within the Republic itself.

The final years of the war of independence helped to push the army away from two of the major ideological streams that competed for influence within the Republic. The catalyst for the army's falling out with Islam was the *Renville* Agreement of early 1948, the second of the abortive attempts at a negotiated settlement. Under the agreement, the Republic conceded to the Dutch the territories which it had lost in mid-1947, including most of West Java, stronghold of the Siliwangi Division; the Division itself was permitted to retreat into Republican areas in Central Java. Left behind in West Java, however, were several important independent Muslim units, which rejected the Republic's authority to concede any of its territory to the Dutch and which decided to continue fighting against colonial rule. When the Siliwangi Division returned to West Java to fight the Dutch after the Dutch attack of late 1948, it found itself also fighting bitterly over territory with these Muslim troops. The affair convinced the army's commanders that radical Muslims were not to be trusted, and recruitment and appointment policies thereafter were designed to ensure that Muslim fundamentalists would not find a base from within the army to launch a claim for political power.

The other ideological stream to lose influence in the armed forces was communism. At the start of the independence struggle, the PKI had chosen a distinctly cautious line, supporting Sjahrir's policy of negotiation and rejecting Tan Malaka's flamboyant calls for mass revolution. More than most political forces of the day, the PKI realised that the key to any kind of programme in independent Indonesia was the survival of the Republican state, and they regarded calls for far-reaching social and economic reform as premature while the Dutch remained to be vanquished. In taking this unpopular line, the PKI willingly deprived itself of a populist platform, but the experience of Tan Malaka showed that this was insufficient as a basis for seizing power. The party, rather, aimed to take gradual control of the state and to win leadership of the independence struggle from within. Its key advantage in this strategy was the defence minister, Amir Sjarifuddin, who became prime minister as well in June 1947 and who had been a secret member of the party since before the war. Sjarifuddin's task, alongside simply strengthening the state, was to strengthen the position of the orthodox Left within the state, especially within the armed forces. He attempted to do this both by favouring units which were ideologically sympathetic to the Left and by installing a network of political education officers throughout the armed forces to train officers and men in ideological orthodoxy. Both strategies put serious strain on the previously cordial relationship between Sjarifuddin and Nasution, because political patronage undermined the respect for military hierarchy which Nasution was attempting to inculcate.

Sjarifuddin's strategy, however, was abruptly thwarted when popular antagonism to the *Renville* Agreement in early 1948 forced him to resign and Sukarno took the opportunity to disregard parliamentary accountability and appointed vice-president Hatta in his place. Hatta's accession coincided with a period of immense hardship and growing political tension in the Republic. Confined to a narrow, overpopulated segment of Central and East Java, the Republic was critically short of food and materials. To conserve the government's limited resources, Hatta embarked on an austerity campaign which included the dismissal of government officials and the disbanding of armed units. These measures fell especially severely on the officials and units which had previously enjoyed Sjarifuddin's patronage, and a growing sense of grievance embittered the already tense political environment. Deprived of access to the institutions of state, the PKI turned to popular appeal to salvage its position, embracing for the first time a programme of radical social reform and uncompromising confrontation with the Dutch. Its new-found radicalism took on greater sharpness with the return from the Soviet Union of Musso, who had been a party leader at the time of the abortive 1926–27 uprisings. The party's secret members, including Sjarifuddin, revealed their affiliation and the party began a determined campaign amongst the workers and peasants of the Republic.

Events stumbled over each other as 1948 wore on. Strikes paralysed government enterprises and clashes began to break out between left- and right-wing armed units. Finally in the East Java town of Madiun a series of escalating incidents and provocations on either side culminated in a coup by the local PKI and the formation of a communist local government.[6] The Hatta government denounced the coup as an uprising against the state. Faced with a choice between denouncing their own people and confronting Hatta, Musso and Sjarifuddin sided with the rebels, accused the Hatta government of betraying the ideals of the revolution and announced a full-scale communist uprising. Brutal civil war followed, during which the bitterness of the preceding months and the profound disappointment with the fruits of independence were unleashed in a series of massacres by Right and Left. Within a month, however, the Left was defeated. Musso was killed, while Sjarifuddin and other leftist leaders were arrested, only to be summarily executed by government forces during the Dutch attack of December 1948.

The Madiun affair left communism, like Islam, with a taint of betrayal which made it permanently suspect in the eyes of the army leadership. But it was only the most spectacular incident of a process of political polarisation which began with the social revolutions at the start of the war of independence. Indonesians had not only tasted independence, they had tasted something of what each of the major ideological streams in the country had to offer by way of practical government. The experience was a chilling one, and the stakes of politics grew higher.

6. Anderson D C 1976 'The Military Aspects of the Madiun Affair'. *Indonesia* 21: 1–64.

CHAPTER THREE
Towards a Unitary Indonesia

The transfer of sovereignty in December 1949 marked the formal end of the struggle for independence, but it was not an unqualified victory for Indonesian nationalism. The agreements accompanying the transfer provided for Indonesia and the Netherlands to form a constitutional Union, for the Republic to take over much of the debt of the former Netherlands Indies, and for the Republic to guarantee that Dutch business could continue to operate freely in Indonesia. Earlier in 1949, moreover, the Dutch had decided unilaterally to separate Western New Guinea from Indonesia and to retain colonial control there. Indonesians watched the transfer of sovereignty, therefore, with a strong feeling that the struggle, although largely won, was not yet over.

In the face of these vestiges of colonialism, the new Republic sought to gather its strength by re-emphasising national unity. During the long struggle for independence, nationalists had seen unity as the key to eventual success, and by 1949 national unity had acquired a special, almost religious appeal for many Indonesians. Politicians such as Sukarno, indeed, put it at the centre of their political ideas and worked to ensure that a single political system would prevail over the whole of Indonesia and over all Indonesians. This pursuit of unity, however, not only led to immediate tension in many regions but further raised the stakes of national politics, making the parliamentary arena in Jakarta the only forum in which different ethnic, cultural and religious groups could lawfully defend their interests.

REGIONS

The first target of this campaign for unification was the political system formally agreed upon in the Dutch–Indonesian negotiations of 1949. The system was federal, the state whose independence the Netherlands recognised in December 1949 being the Republik Indonesia Serikat, or Republic of the United States of Indonesia (RUSI).[1] The RUSI comprised sixteen states: the Republic of Indonesia and the fifteen members of the former BFO.[2] The Republic of Indonesia was by far the most powerful of these states. Its army was to be the core of the new federal army, and its leaders, Sukarno and Hatta, were unquestionably the best known political leaders in the federation. The BFO states themselves varied in size, status and degree of political and social integrity. The State of East Indonesia had a population of ten million, a lively parliament and an incipient army; the so-called 'Neo-land' of Riau had a population of around 100,000 and virtually no political institutions of its own.

For most Republican leaders, federalism was a Dutch strategy to preserve as much influence as possible by keeping Indonesia divided and weak – a kind of post-colonial policy of divide and rule. They accepted it, therefore, only as a means of securing Dutch recognition of their independence and had no intention of allowing it to survive.

Even within the BFO states, political opinion by no means unanimously supported the federal system. In some regions, Dutch rule had been re-established in the teeth of local nationalist opposition, and this nationalism, though suppressed, had not been extinguished. With the ending of the armed struggle, moreover, many Indonesians from the BFO regions who had served the Republic, or who had been political prisoners in Dutch jails, returned to their homes bringing with them their republican loyalties. And as Dutch power receded, many BFO leaders found it prudent to shift their allegiances towards the Republic.

Almost as soon as the Dutch flag was lowered over the governor-general's palace in Jakarta for the last time, therefore, nationalists

1. This is the official English translation of the state's name, although Federal Republic of Indonesia would more accurately convey the meaning of the Indonesian language title.
2. The abbreviation stood for Bijeenkomst voor Federaal Overleg, or Federal Consultative Assembly, into which these states had been grouped before the recognition of independence.

began agitating to have the federal system replaced by a unitary structure. During the first seven months of 1950, the governments of the BFO states bowed, one by one, to this pressure and dissolved their states into the Republic. On 17 August 1950, the fifth anniversary of the proclamation of independence, Sukarno announced that the federal system had been abolished and the unitary republic restored. For the most part the dissolution of federalism proceeded without great drama. In only a few regions was there any serious opposition: West Java, West Kalimantan and East Indonesia. Of these, the East Indonesia case stands out as the most important, because only here did substantial resistance to the re-establishment of the unitary state continue for any length of time. This resistance had two major geographical focuses.

In South Sulawesi, especially around the main city, Makasar (now Ujung Pandang), there was considerable support for the federal system from local political leaders and from the commanders of the substantial body of KNIL[3] troops stationed in and around the city. In early April a force of ex-KNIL soldiers under the leadership of Captain Andi Abdul Aziz attacked central government units in the city and placed their leaders under arrest. The position which the government of East Indonesia took towards these developments might perhaps most generously be described as ambivalent. The central government, however, denounced Aziz and ordered him to appear in Jakarta at once. He eventually complied, and on arrival was placed under arrest. Central government troops then landed in Makasar and soon brought the remaining rebel forces under control.

The second focus of opposition to the unitary state was Ambon, where the Dutch had traditionally recruited many soldiers and where Dutch influence remained strong. Several members of the government of East Indonesia had fled there after the collapse of the Andi Aziz coup attempt and continued resistance to the dismantling of the RUSI. Former KNIL soldiers were again prominent in these developments, providing the civilian leaders with the military backing which made resistance to the central government possible. On 25 April 1950, these leaders proclaimed the independence of the Republic of the South Moluccas (Republik Maluku Selatan: RMS). The central government initially tried to negotiate with the RMS leaders, but to no avail. Eventually, in July, military action was launched against the rebels. By the end

---

3. Koninklijk Nederlands Indisch Leger: Royal Netherlandsch Indies Army.

of December the rebellion had been defeated, though some RMS supporters managed to flee to the Netherlands.

These risings against the Republic severely damaged the already tattered political reputation of federalism, but the notion that the Republic should take special account of regional identities in its political structure was dealt a further sharp blow by Dutch policy over western New Guinea. The western half of the island of New Guinea[4] had been the last major part of the colony of Netherlands Indies to fall under Dutch control. Apart from a few oil wells on the Bird's Head Peninsula, in 1940 the only major use the Dutch made of the territory was as the site for a prison camp for political detainees. This camp, called Tanah Merah[5] and located on the Digul River 300 kilometres north of Merauke, had housed many prominent Indonesian nationalist leaders, including Hatta and Sjahrir. This gave the territory added significance in nationalist mythology.

Until 1948 the Dutch had clearly regarded western New Guinea as an integral part of the Netherlands Indies. During the last two years of the independence struggle, however, forces in the Netherlands began pressing the government in The Hague to separate the territory from the rest of the colony. They argued that the island was culturally and ethnically distinct from the rest of Indonesia. They also felt that Dutch prestige would be irreparably harmed if the whole of the colony were 'given away'. And they suggested that the region could provide a homeland for the Eurasians who were expected to leave, or would perhaps be expelled from, Indonesia after the recognition of sovereignty.

The Republican government in Yogyakarta and its counterparts in the BFO states were united in arguing strongly that the territory should not be separated from the rest of the country. Eventually, neither the Indonesians nor the Dutch being willing to budge, the Round Table Conference agreed that the status quo with respect to the territory should be preserved temporarily, pending the final

4. The Dutch referred to the territory as Nieuw-Guinea and it was known internationally as Dutch New Guinea or West New Guinea. The Republic initially called the region Irian Barat or West Irian, the name Irian being derived from a local word meaning 'shimmering land'. In 1972 this name was changed to Irian Jaya ('Victorious Irian'). Local resistance movements to Indonesian rule call the region West Papua.

5. This was its Indonesian name: the Dutch name was Boven Digul. There was also a second camp, further upstream, called Tanah Tinggi for the so-called 'irreconcilables', those prisoners who refused all instructions from the prison authorities.

resolution of the matter within twelve months of the recognition of Indonesia's independence. In fact, although extensive discussions on the matter took place during 1950, and then into 1951, no resolution of the issue was reached. As the Dutch began to develop a political infrastructure and to talk of eventual separate independence for the territory, Indonesian opposition to separate regional political identity became further entrenched.

As well as dismantling federalism, the Republic moved to reform the complicated system of local and regional government inherited from the Dutch. So-called 'self-governing territories' – the 282 formerly independent indigenous states which had a variety of treaty relationships with the Dutch – were fitted into a three-tiered system of administration: province, *kabupaten* (regency) and village.[6] The Sultanate of Yogyakarta, which had played a special role in the struggle against the Dutch, was made into a province, with its traditional ruler, Sultan Hamengku Buwono IX, as governor for life.[7] In most cases, however, the self-governing territories were made equivalent to *kabupaten* or were federated into *kabupaten*. The separate courts which had administered law in the self-governing territories during the colonial era were abolished and their duties taken over by national courts. Many of the judges who had formerly sat in these courts were taken into the government judiciary, even though they often had minimal experience of the national legal system and of the laws they were now expected to apply. Traditional rulers continued to govern their regions, while ostensibly now acting as officials in a national system of administration. Jakarta, nevertheless, intended this condition to be temporary; it thus moved gradually to divest the regions and their traditional rulers of their special status, and to transform them into 'normal' units of administration, with their heads selected according to national practice.

Administrative authority over the regions, too, was tightened. The central government recognised in theory that a country as diverse as Indonesia needed to devolve some power to sub-national units of government, if only to make government workable. In 1948 the Republican government enacted legislation to devolve some political decision-making power to the regions. The three levels of administration were to have elected councils with specific

6. Municipalities were also second-level districts, on a par with *kabupaten*.
7. Special District status, equivalent to that of a province, was also accorded to the Jakarta Municipality.

responsibilities assigned to them. They would be headed by an official selected by the central government from a list of between two and four candidates nominated by the councils. The unitary state took over this legislation on its establishment in 1950. The way the legislation was implemented, however, differed from the letter of the law. Most important, taking advantage of a transitional escape clause, the central government decided that for the moment it would appoint regional heads directly, rather than through the consultative method formally required. The people so appointed were almost invariably members of the central government's territorial administrative service, the *pamong praja*.[8] And the powers to be delegated to the regional councils were tightly circumscribed, allowing the regions little opportunity to exercise independent political decision-making.

The crucially important area of education is a good example. The regions had been promised some autonomy but in practice this autonomy extended only to matters such as providing the infrastructure for the educational system – the school buildings and so forth – and nothing else. There was no question of the provinces, for instance, being able to set their own school curricula, train their own teachers, adopt their own textbooks or use a language other than Indonesian in their schools.[9] On all these matters, the central government's authority remained absolute. This common educational experience helped to create a national culture, shared by the generations of Indonesians growing up after 1949.

Only at the village level was the central government's concern for uniformity of administration relatively weak. The traditional village system of justice, *adat*, was allowed to continue. This had the effect of keeping the legal system in touch with the population at large, and enabled communities where this law was practised to retain the capacity to make decisions for themselves on legal matters specific to the community. But national law prevailed over *adat*, so villages had jurisdiction only over a limited range of matters.

8. The term *pamong praja* literally means servants of the state or realm. Under the Dutch, the term had been slightly but significantly different: *pangreh praja*, or rulers of the state. The change was symbolically important, though whether in fact it represented any real change in the relations between these people and the people in the territories under their control is another matter.

9. The only minor exception to the use of Indonesian was that a local language could be used for the first three years of primary school.

A final conclusive sign that few concessions were to be offered to regional identity came as preparations were made slowly for Indonesia's first national elections. These elections, for a parliament and for a Constituent Assembly which would draw up a permanent constitution to replace the interim constitution adopted in August 1950, were seen as providing formal, popular legitimacy for the state whose structure had thus far been determined by political and military leaders whose popular followings were unproven. The system of proportional representation chosen, however, effectively treated the entire country as a single electorate, giving the inhabitants of Java, who numbered well over half the country's population, the power to dominate at election time.

RELIGION

The new Republican government was equally unwilling to allow any of its citizens special consideration on grounds of religion, and it rejected especially the idea of an Islamic state. Islamic doctrine gives the state a central role in enforcing Islamic law and practices and in creating an Islamic society. To have made Indonesia an Islamic state, however, or even to have accepted the Jakarta Charter, which would have obliged the state to impose Islamic law on all its Muslim citizens, would have interfered drastically with the religious observance of the nominally Muslim followers of Kejawen and would have left Christians and other religious minorities feeling like second-class citizens. Even many political leaders who were devoutly Islamic in their personal lives, such as Vice-President Muhammad Hatta, recognised the validity of this argument. After briefly agreeing with the inclusion of the Jakarta Charter in the constitution, Hatta took the initiative to have it removed when the constitution was formally presented to the provisional parliament for ratification on 18 August 1945. The Preamble to the 1945 Constitution noted that the Republic of Indonesia was based on the principle of Belief in the One Supreme God, the first of the Five Principles of the Pancasila. The God referred to, however, was not just the God of Islam, and the state was not to be an Islamic one. Both the federal constitution of 1949 and the interim unitary constitution of 1950 took the same position as the original constitution of 1945. The only significant concession to Islam was the retention of Islamic courts with jurisdiction over family law, mainly marriage, inheritance and divorce. These courts were a legacy of the colonial era, when the Dutch had sought to reconcile Muslims to foreign rule by supporting religious observance and customs as long as they were not directed against the state.

A modified federal system might have partly accommodated orthodox Muslim demands because the strongest adherence to orthodoxy was in a few regions such as Aceh, West Java and South Sulawesi. In the unitary state, however, the only lawful avenue for orthodox Muslims who sought the political changes their faith required was national politics in Jakarta, through the national parliament and the planned Constituent Assembly, whose task would be to draw up a permanent constitution for the state.

For some Muslims, however, such forums were too uncertain; they took their struggle outside these confines, and directly challenged the state. The movements they led are commonly referred to as the Darul Islam.[10] The Darul Islam uprising began in West Java in 1948 when the Republic agreed with the Dutch to withdraw its regular troops, the elite Siliwangi Division, from the region. This decision incensed local Islamic political leaders who saw themselves as being abandoned to infidel rule. Backed by military units of the Hizbullah, a military force associated with the Masjumi political party, they proclaimed Islamic rule in the region under the leadership of S. M. Kartosoewirjo and vowed to continue the armed struggle against the Dutch. When the Siliwangi began moving back into West Java after the Dutch attack of late 1948, the Republic began to confront the Muslim rebels directly.

After the transfer of sovereignty had removed the Dutch, the Republic tried to negotiate a settlement with the Darul Islam. Kartosoewirjo, however, consistently refused to meet the representatives of the central government, with the result that Jakarta lost its patience and commenced military operations against the rebels. The struggle was difficult, because the Darul Islam was backed by experienced guerrilla fighters and operated in rugged terrain where it was able to count on the support of the local people, initially voluntary, though later more by coercion. By the mid 1950s, although the major towns and cities of West Java were securely in government hands, the countryside was not, and the steep and winding sections of the road from Jakarta to Bandung needed to be patrolled constantly to protect traffic from attacks.

10. Literally, 'world or territory of Islam'. For a good discussion of the origins of the Darul Islam movements, see van Dijk C 1981 *Rebellion under the Banner of Islam* (Martinus Nijhoff, The Hague), especially Chapter 1.

By this time, however, the Islamic revolt had spread further afield, to regions including South Sulawesi and Aceh. In South Sulawesi, the crushing of the Andi Aziz revolt did not resolve tensions created by the presence of a large number of local guerrilla fighters, the bulk of whom the central government wanted to see demobilised and absorbed back in civilian society.[11] Only a few of them – perhaps as few as 4,000 – were to be taken into the new national army. Many guerrilla leaders rejected this proposal, seeing it as a move to assert central government authority over their region, and also to reduce their own standing: they were undoubtedly correct on both counts. The formal break with Jakarta came in 1951, when troops under Kahar Muzakkar left Makasar and took to the hills, hours before they were to be incorporated into the national army. In January 1952 Kahar Muzakkar announced that he had accepted the position of Darul Islam commander for Sulawesi, thus formally linking his movement with that of Kartosoewirjo. As in West Java, the central government responded with a military push against the rebels, although initially with limited success.

The revolt in Aceh was even more serious. The Acehnese were – and are – renowned for the strength of their devotion to Islam. Neither the Dutch nor the Japanese had ever managed fully to conquer the region; in 1945 Acehnese leaders had declared the area as part of the Republic, but the Republican government had a very limited capacity to influence events there. Indeed, it could do so really only to the extent that local leaders permitted.

In 1947 a leading Acehnese religious figure, Daud Beureu'eh, was appointed the Republican military governor of the province of North Sumatra, including Aceh. Nearly two years later, in late 1948 and early 1949, Daud Beureu'eh demanded formal recognition of Aceh as a separate province. The Republican government at this time was operating on an emergency basis from Padang in West Sumatra, its headquarters in Yogyakarta and most of its key personnel having been captured by the Dutch. It was in a weakened political position, and had little choice but to accede to the Acehnese demand. Daud Beureu'eh, not surprisingly, was appointed as Aceh's governor.

After August 1950, the Republican government sought to reassert its authority by downgrading the status of Aceh, re-

11. The numbers of troops involved is not known with certainty, although Feith suggests they numbered around 20,000. See Feith H 1963 *The Decline of Constitutional Democracy in Indonesia* (Cornell University Press, Ithaca), p. 212.

incorporating it into the province of North Sumatra. The central government also moved to consolidate its power by replacing religious leaders who had occupied civil government positions during the armed struggle with members of the local aristocracy, the *uleëbalang*.[12] Alienated from the central government, the religious leaders struck out against Jakarta, portraying it as a hotbed of political, moral and economic corruption and alleging that it treated Aceh shabbily in funding public works such as roads, irrigation systems and educational facilities. But the crucial issue was still Islam.

In early 1953 Sukarno visited Aceh, to be greeted by large crowds demonstrating against the Pancasila and in favour of Islam as the basis of the state. Later during the same year the central government alleged that its forces had found evidence of clandestine communications between Daud Beureu'eh and the Darul Islam in West Java. In this atmosphere of confrontation, in September 1953 Daud Beureu'eh proclaimed Aceh's secession from the Republic of Indonesia, and its adherence to the Indonesian Islamic State of the Darul Islam. The proclamation was marked by a series of attacks on army and government posts by Islamic guerrilla groups.

Thus, in attempting to resolve the question of Islam's place in society, the central government drove large numbers of its subjects into full scale revolt. Although the central government's handling of the Islamic issue was sometimes insensitive, the problem was basically intractable. Greater concessions to Islam might have conciliated the Acehnese, but would have alienated other religious groups, including Christians and the Javanese followers of Kejawen. The Darul Islam revolt seriously weakened the Republic in the short term, but had the long-term effect of strengthening the argument that the central government should be able to disregard the concerns, and even the deeply held convictions, of important social groups in the interests of the state.

RACE

In dealing with the regions and with religious groups, the new Indonesian government was keen to assert the power of the

12. The *uleëbalang* had been engaged in a long struggle with these religious leaders since at least the eighteenth century, and had often filled the role of agents of outside forces, the Dutch, the Japanese and now the central government.

centre and the principle of equality for all. In their policy, however, towards Indonesia's Chinese minority, the Republic's leaders were more ambivalent. They were uncertain whether Indonesia's interests would be best served by including them fully in the new polity or limiting their citizenship in various ways.

Unease over the Chinese had a political and an economic background. Few Chinese in Indonesia had been involved in the Indonesian nationalist movement, whereas a significant number been actively involved in the Chinese nationalist cause. Ethnic Chinese, moreover, had played a more prominent and profitable role in the colonial economy than indigenous Indonesians. Many indigenous Indonesians, therefore, were suspicious of Chinese political loyalties and concerned that the Chinese might use the removal of the Dutch as an opportunity to strengthen their economic power.

The constitutions of 1949 and 1950 provided for the legal equality of all Indonesian citizens. In a number of respects, however, the racial distinction of the colonial period was maintained. Chinese family law remained valid. Candidacy for the office of president was restricted to citizens who were *asli*, a term which was widely interpreted to mean indigenous Indonesians, thus excluding Indonesians of Chinese descent. And the Agrarian Law of 1870, which limited ownership of land to indigenous Indonesians, remained in force.

By far the most important area of concern to ethnic Chinese, however, was citizenship.[13] Since 1910 Chinese born in the Indies of parents who were themselves resident in the Indies had legally been Dutch subjects (though not Dutch citizens). By 1930, two-thirds of all ethnic Chinese in the Indies were second- (or subsequent) generation immigrants, and thus prima facie Dutch subjects. In 1909, however, China had enacted legislation providing that any child of a Chinese father or mother was a citizen of China, no matter where it was born. Thus at the end of the colonial era, most ethnic Chinese in the Indies were both Dutch subjects and Chinese citizens.

Shortly after the proclamation of independence, the provisional parliament adopted legislation granting citizenship to non-indigenous people so long as they had been born in Indonesia, had resided there consecutively for the previous five years, were aged

13. Arabs, Indians and Europeans (including Eurasians) were also affected by citizenship legislation, but their numbers were small compared with those of the Chinese.

at least twenty-one years (or were married), and had not rejected Indonesian citizenship in favour of the citizenship of another country. The system was thus a passive one: unless they took positive action to the contrary, ethnic Chinese who fulfilled the residential and age requirements automatically became Indonesian citizens. This did not, however, mean that they ceased to be regarded by China as Chinese citizens: in fact they held dual Indonesian and Chinese nationality. Essentially the same arrangement was adopted by the RUSI and the unitary Republic. Many members of the Indonesian parliament – probably the majority of them – suspected that the Chinese were loyal either to the Netherlands or to China, but not to Indonesia. Given the economic strength of the Chinese community, however, it was important for the Republic to secure Chinese sympathy and support. Making Indonesian citizenship available to them fairly readily was one move in this direction.

It is not entirely clear how many ethnic Chinese became Indonesian citizens through this process. The best estimate, however, is that out of a Chinese population of about 2.1 million in 1950, about 1.5 million were born in Indonesia of whom 390,000 rejected Indonesian citizenship within the two years permitted. This would mean that about 1.1 million ethnic Chinese became Indonesian citizens, or just over half the ethnic Chinese population.

This passive system of citizenship, with its inherent acceptance of dual Indonesian–Chinese nationality, was not particularly popular amongst indigenous political leaders because it permitted a class of citizens whose ultimate loyalty to Indonesia could be doubted. Soon after the recognition of independence, therefore, many of Indonesia's politicians began to push for a review of the citizenship law to try to force the ethnic Chinese to make a clear choice between Indonesia and China. Their ultimate aim was to abolish dual nationality altogether.

Little could be done in 1950 to achieve this goal, because the new People's Republic of China retained the policies of earlier Chinese governments which made it extremely difficult for Chinese citizens to renounce their nationality.[14] Until the PRC changed its position, Indonesia could not alter the fact that ethnic Chinese in Indonesia

14. The Nationalist government on Taiwan took the same view on this matter as the PRC government, but Indonesia had no diplomatic relations with the Nationalists, and the issue was of less consequence.

had Chinese citizenship – whether or not at the same time they held Indonesian citizenship. Only in February 1954 did gradually warming relations between Jakarta and Beijing encourage the Ali Sastroamidjojo government to introduce a Bill which would shift from a passive system for the acquisition of Indonesian citizenship to an active system. In order to retain Indonesian citizenship, ethnic Chinese now had to satisfy two criteria in addition to the ones they had had to fulfil in 1949: they had to prove that their parents were born in Indonesia and had lived there for a minimum of ten years; and they had to renounce their Chinese citizenship. The first clause was intended to exclude from citizenship those Chinese whose closer family ties with China might make them less loyal, but the second clause was the crucial one in establishing who was and who was not a citizen. It depended on the cooperation of the PRC for its implementation and in April 1954 Beijing indicated its willingness to negotiate on this point. These negotiations took a year, but they resulted, in 1955, in the signing by the foreign ministers of the two countries of a Dual Nationality Treaty.

The treaty provided that, before 1 January 1962, all Indonesians holding Chinese citizenship had to decide whether to reject such citizenship. They were assumed to have retained Chinese citizenship unless they acted positively to reject it. And retention of Chinese citizenship was to be incompatible with continuing to hold Indonesian citizenship.[15] Anyone born after 1960 would be assumed automatically to hold the citizenship of his or her father.

Ironically, before this treaty had been concluded, the Ali government had withdrawn the proposed Nationality Law. The proposal had come under strong attack, in particular from *peranakan*[16] Chinese leaders, who protested at having to go through yet another process in order to confirm or assert their Indonesian citizenship. The communist party, on which the cabinet depended for support in parliament, also expressed reservations about the Bill.

In the area of citizenship, therefore, the Republic failed to establish its boundaries unambiguously, and the Chinese com-

15. The only major exception was in the case of ethnic Chinese children who had up until their eighteenth birthday to make the choice, even if this fell after 1 January 1962. Given that such people probably made up one-third of the total ethnic Chinese community, this meant that the citizenship issue was likely to continue to be a matter of considerable significance for some time after 1962.

16. Those ethnic Chinese whose primary cultural orientation was to Indonesia, not China.

munities were thus left with an uncomfortable intermediate status, not unlike their position under colonialism. Resident in Indonesia but saddled with Chinese citizenship whether they wanted it or not, Chinese Indonesians were expected to show unqualified loyalty to the Republic, yet were often treated as foreigners. The 'Benteng' ('Fortress') programme, for instance, which gave indigenous Indonesians priority in the allocation of import licences, was intended to strengthen indigenous control of the economy at the expense of Chinese Indonesians. The programme was never particularly successful, but this was more the result of inefficiency and concern for the programme's overall effects on the economy than because of any consideration for the Chinese.

One side effect of this ambiguity was the formation in March 1954 of Baperki, the Consultative Body on Indonesian Citizenship. Although formally not attached to any ethnic group, Baperki was quickly recognised as the major political representative of *peranakan* Chinese. It evolved into a powerful organisation, fielding candidates in the 1955 elections (though winning only one seat), establishing Indonesian-medium schools and colleges for ethnic Chinese and generally expressing the views of the *peranakan* community more forcefully and effectively than ever before. In particular, Baperki promoted the idea of the integration of the Chinese community into the broader Indonesian community, not its assimilation into that community. Essentially this meant that the Chinese would be recognised as one of the many ethnic groups which made up Indonesian society, alongside the Javanese, the Balinese and so forth. One could be ethnic Chinese and a good Indonesian citizen, Baperki argued, just as one could be an ethnic Javanese and a good Indonesian: there was no inherent clash between these two ideas. The assimilationists argued to the contrary, that since the Chinese as an ethnic group were not indigenous to Indonesia, they could not be recognised on the same level as the ethnic groups which were indigenous, and thus that they had to let go all elements of Chinese culture in order to be accepted as Indonesian. Generally speaking, until the change of government in the mid 1960s, it was the integrationist approach which was officially followed by Indonesian governments, though in practice several governments adopted policies which appeared to move in the reverse direction.

CONCLUSION

By the mid 1950s, the efforts to unify the Indonesian state had met with mixed results. Many of the divisive elements the Indonesian state had inherited from its colonial predecessor had been eliminated. With some exceptions, formal discrimination on the grounds of race or ethnicity had been struck out. A national culture which embraced (or included) Indonesians from various ethnic and religious backgrounds was in the process of being created. A state structure had been created which provided for a unitary system of government, involving the uniform application of national laws, regulations and patterns of administration across the country. By gathering political authority to the centre in this way, however, the Republic made Jakarta the focus of politics as it had never been before. The multitude of aspirations for an independent Indonesia kindled by the years of struggle now came together in the parliament to decide the future of the country.

CHAPTER FOUR

Party Dominance, 1950–55

The parliament which met in Jakarta in 1950 was a hybrid affair, the product of four years of turbulent politics in the Republic and of the hasty dismantling of the federal government. It was not elected, but its membership was broad enough to provide a voice to all the important political streams and cultural groups. This diversity was both its greatest strength and its greatest weakness.

When nationalist leaders originally planned the political structure of the Republic in the final disturbed weeks of the Japanese occupation, their commitment to unity had led them to draft a constitution with a strong executive presidency. The president had the power to appoint and dismiss cabinet ministers, who were responsible to him rather than to the parliament; the president was also the commander-in-chief of the armed forces. The parliament was to consist of two chambers. The People's Consultative Assembly (MPR) would meet only once every five years to elect the president.[1] The smaller People's Representative Council (DPR), all of whose members also belonged to the MPR, would meet more frequently, but would share with the president the right to initiate legislation. The president, moreover, was empowered to veto legislation passed by the Council. This constitution was adopted by the Preparatory Committee for Indonesian Independence on 18 August 1945, the day after the proclamation of independence. As we have seen, Sukarno

---

1. It was also entrusted with formulating the so-called Broad Outlines of State Policy (Garis Besar Haluan Negara) which were to guide governments during the five-year parliamentary term.

was elected the nation's first president, and Muhammad Hatta its first vice-president.

The Preparatory Committee further enhanced the powers of the president by deciding that, pending national parliamentary elections, the functions assigned to the parliament could be exercised by the president assisted by a Central Indonesian National Committee (Komite Nasional Indonesia Pusat: KNIP) which he was to appoint. Furthermore, it was agreed that for six months, the president had overriding responsibility to organise and manage all the institutions and functions set out in the constitution. And finally, it was agreed that Sukarno and Hatta should head a single state party, to be called the Partai Nasional Indonesia (Indonesian National Party), through which all political activities would be channelled.

This extreme concentration of power in the hands of the president did not last long. Although President Sukarno had wider political support than any other leader, by no means all Indonesians were happy to see him with such far-reaching powers. They were disturbed, too, by his choice of ministers for the Republic's first cabinet, most of them members of the modernising nationalist stream who had cooperated with the Japanese during the war. Large sections of Indonesian public opinion, notably organised Islam and the Left, were apparently being excluded from a say in the decision-making of the new state. All the more alarming was the fact that the close connections of Sukarno and his cabinet with the Japanese seemed likely to damage the Republic's campaign for international recognition.

Accordingly, a coalition of politicised youth groups (*pemuda*) and leftists, many of whom had spent the war years in jail or in hiding, began to press for changes which would both open the political system to wider participation and distance the Republic from the Japanese. The force of their arguments was so great that the authoritarian, centralised political system of the 1945 constitution began to be pulled down only weeks after it had been proclaimed. Restive political groups began to form their own parties despite the government ban. In October 1945, Vice-President Hatta who, although he had worked with the Japanese, was also a Marxist and convinced of the need to give the Republic impeccable democratic credentials, issued a proclamation that the provisional powers previously allotted to the president would now be exercised by the KNIP, via a Working Committee, soon to be established.[2] The ministers in the cabinet, formerly responsible only to the president, were now to be responsible to the Working Committee. The Working Committee itself was set up shortly after: it was headed by Sutan Sjahrir, who became prime minister. Early the next month, the government rescinded the earlier decision to establish a state party – which had never got off the ground anyway – and acknowledged the right of all Indonesians to form their own political parties.

The effect of these decisions was to produce a political system which was parliamentary rather than presidential. The KNIP was based on the old, Japanese-appointed Preparatory Committee, but its membership was broadened to 200 to ensure that all regions and major political streams were represented and the Working Committee was drawn from these on a proportional basis. Members of parliament were by and large grouped into parties and a coalition of parties formed the government. Cabinet was headed by a prime minister and was responsible to the KNIP Working Committee for performance of its duties. The rules of the parliamentary system were never specified, and from time to time Sukarno intervened decisively as president to sway the outcome of crucial votes. During 1946 Sukarno's prestige helped preserve Sjahrir as prime minister, despite widespread antagonism towards his negotiations with the Dutch, and in early 1947 the president added 314 new members to the KNIP in order to ensure ratification of the deeply unpopular Linggajati Agreement. In January 1948, moreover, Sukarno appointed Hatta as prime minister over the head of former prime minister Amir Sjarifuddin, even though Hatta did not command a parliamentary majority. Hatta formally retained this position until just before the transfer of sovereignty.[3] Nonetheless, most Indonesians looked on these interventions as temporary departures from the parliamentary system, rather than as signs of its inadequacy, and there was no suggestion in 1949 that Indonesia should revert to a presidential system.

The 1950 interim constitution set up a unicameral parliament with 232 members drawn both from the Republic of Indonesia

2. The Working Committee thus had a relationship to the KNIP similar to that of the DPR to the larger MPR. This system, in which the legislature was drawn from a larger representative body, was derived from the colonial era, when the day-to-day business of the quasi-legislative Volksraad (People's Council) was handled by a smaller representative College of Delegates.

3. He also served as prime minister of the RUSI during the first months of 1950 while federalism was being dismantled.

and from the other federal states, where the Dutch had set up a variety of local parliaments and had also permitted the formation of political parties. Hatta resigned as prime minister in August 1950, but in most salient respects there was little change to the system which had emerged during the struggle against the Dutch. Government was effectively in the hands of a cabinet of ministers, headed by a prime minister. All cabinet ministers, including the prime minister, had to be members of the parliament, to which they were individually and collectively responsible. The cabinet could retain office only as long as it retained the confidence of the parliament.

The position of president, still filled by Sukarno, was ceremonial and symbolic rather than powerful and decisive. The most important political function that the president played was the appointment of a cabinet *formateur* after an election or whenever the fall of a government made a new cabinet necessary. *Formateurs* were responsible for negotiating the make-up of a new cabinet amongst the various parties and factions; they themselves might or might not participate in the cabinets they were forming. Because a new cabinet was needed rather frequently, the right to appoint *formateurs* was of some political significance, but it was minor when compared with the power and influence wielded by the prime minister.

Political parties were central elements in this political system. Of the sixteen parties represented in the parliament, the largest was the Muslim party, Masjumi, followed by the Partai Nasional Indonesia (Indonesian Nationalist Party, PNI), the Partai Indonesia Raja (Greater Indonesia Party, PIR) and the Partai Sosialis Indonesia (Indonesian Socialist Party, PSI). Even the Masjumi, however, held only forty-nine seats, just 21 per cent of the total. The PNI controlled thirty-six seats, and the PIR and the PSI each seventeen seats. The so-called Democratic Fraction, whose members were drawn from the former BFO state parliaments, had thirteen seats, as did the Partai Komunis Indonesia (Indonesian Communist Party, PKI). Amongst the smaller parties, the Catholic Party held nine seats, the Protestant Partai Kristen Indonesia (Parkindo) five and the Partai Sarekat Islam Indonesia (PSII) five. There were also two seats held by the Peasants' Group, and twenty-six by independent members.

By 1955 both the composition and the number of the parties had changed as a result of changes in party allegiance. Masjumi (forty-four seats) had suffered the secession of the Nahdatul

Ulama (eight seats), but was still the largest party in parliament by a narrow margin. The PNI had grown to forty-two and the PKI to seventeen, while the PSI had shrunk to fourteen. The PIR had grown by one, the Catholics and the PSII had dropped by one, and Parkindo was steady on five. The party system, however, remained much the same.

These political parties were rather different creatures from those in Western political culture. In the West, the term political party generally implies an organisation created to promote a particular ideological viewpoint and to win representation in parliament by directly appealing to voters at election time. Indonesia's political parties, by contrast, were much more loosely tied to defined ideological positions. As we have seen, the thinking of most nationalists drew to varying degrees from socialism, religion, notions of modernisation and ideas of cultural revival; whatever the principles proclaimed by a party's name therefore – Islam, socialism, nationalism, and so on – most of the larger parties encompassed a wide range of ideological opinions and political styles. The strength of the parties, moreover, was generally not based on a direct appeal to the public but rather on negotiation with existing social formations and loyalties. Party supporters, and even party members, responded less to their national leaders, manifestos and party organisations than to local power-brokers: religious, ethnic and cultural leaders, power-holders in local government, union organisers and the like – and the ordinary members of each party often had virtually no say in deciding the platforms the parties would adopt, or the people who would lead them. As organisations independent of this social base, the parties were exceptionally weak and were often little more than creatures of their leaders. On the other hand, during the 1950s they were also the main political expression of deep-seated cultural and social streams in Indonesian society. As long as they continued to cultivate this social base, they could be very strong indeed.

As a result, Indonesian political parties showed an often bewildering mix of obduracy and opportunism. They were capable of cynical and unprincipled horse-trading ('cow-trading' in Indonesian parlance), especially over access to government posts and funds, but they could also mount an implacable and destructive campaign of resistance when the convictions of their backers were at stake. Politics slid therefore between fluid, self-serving factionalism and rigid ideological polarisation. In analysing the relationship of the parties with each other, one can focus on ideology and social base or on practical political orientation, but the two are often difficult to reconcile.

IDEOLOGIES AND SOCIAL BASES OF THE PARTIES

The majority of the parties fall ideologically into three groupings: those based on religion, those based on socialism, and those based on avowedly indigenous nationalism.[4]

Religious parties

The largest of the religiously-based parties was the Masjumi, the party of Islamic modernism.[5] The modernist or reformist wing of Islam believed that the faith should be restored to its original purity by removal of all the interpretations placed on the Qur'an by human beings, interpretations which, in the eyes of modernists, had obscured the teachings of the Prophet Muhammad. Since the Prophet's teachings were timeless, this would mean restoring Islam to a modern form, and rescuing it from the Middle Ages, when many of these man-made interpretations of the faith had been created. For the modernists, doctrinal purification was essential if Islamic societies were to overcome their subordinate position in the world and to deliver the benefits of modernity to their subjects.

The Masjumi's statutes declared that the aim of the party was: 'implementation of the teachings and laws of Islam in the life of individuals, society and the Indonesian Republican State'.[6]

Its leaders differed in the extent to which they saw an Islamic state as an achievable goal, but they shared at least the belief that

4. This three-fold division is a useful one, but certainly not the only way of dividing up the parties. A slightly different way is presented in Feith H and Castles L (eds) 1970 *Indonesian Political Thinking 1945–1965* (Cornell University Press, Ithaca). Feith and Castles divide the parties according to five 'streams of thought': radical nationalism, Javanese traditionalism, Islam, democratic socialism and communism. The authors also ingeniously plot the position of the main parties and streams of thought on a kind of map, from left to right and from traditionalism to Western influence (p. 14).

5. When it was formed on 7 November 1945, the Masjumi included all the major schools of Islamic social and political thought in Indonesia because it inherited both the name and the organisational framework of an umbrella Islamic organisation created by the Japanese during the occupation. By 1952, however, most Muslim traditionalists (discussed below) had abandoned it.

6. Article III, reproduced in Kementerian Penerangan 1954 *Kepartaian dan Parlementaria* (Jakarta), p. 443.

the state should be guided by the ethics of Islam in formulating policy and that it should work to create a society which put no impediment in the path of religious practice for pious Muslims. Its political ideology could perhaps be best described as Islamic social democracy. Although the Masjumi formally denied that there was or could be any distinction between secular and religious life, it did not stress this point 'and tended to operate as though there were a degree of independence between the two'.[7] The Masjumi's supporters were to be found particularly among the urban Islamic business community, especially traders and manufacturers of commodities such as cigarettes and textiles. Geographically, the party's major bases were in the ethnically Sundanese region of West Java, and the more heavily Islamised areas of Sumatra and Sulawesi. It was not strong in Central or East Java.

The primary political representative of the traditionalist Muslims was the Nahdatul Ulama (Islamic Scholars' Party). Founded in 1926, the NU had originally been a non-political organisation concerned with issues of social welfare and education. During the Japanese occupation, it had become part of the first Masjumi, and was a founder-member of the Masjumi party in 1945. In 1952, however, following a series of political and religious disagreements with the dominant faction in the Masjumi, the NU broke away from the organisation, and established itself as a separate political party.

In contrast to the modernist Muslims, the traditionalists wanted to maintain the ways in which Islam had traditionally been observed in Indonesia, in particular in Java. Unlike the modernists, they accepted the interpretations of Islam devised by learned Islamic scholars – past and present – as a legitimate part of the faith. Moreover, although their religious practice was far closer to orthodox Islam than that of the nominally Muslim followers of Kejawen, they nonetheless maintained a number of beliefs which owed much to Hinduism and Buddhism as they had been practised in Java.

It is difficult to specify just what the NU's political ideology was. Like the Masjumi, the NU refrained from campaigning publicly for an Islamic state, noting simply that it sought: 'implementation of the laws of Islam in society'.[8]

7. Clifford Geertz, cited in Legge J D 1980 *Indonesia* (3rd edn; Prentice-Hall of Australia, Sydney), p. 65.
8. Article II b, reproduced in Kementerian Penerangan 1954 *Kepartaian dan Parlementaria*, p. 414.

It aimed like the Masjumi for a state which at least placed no impediment in the path of Islam, but unlike the Masjumi it had no broad vision for modernising society. Indeed, in a significant sense, it did not have a specifically *political* ideology: its ideology was Islam. The party has been accused of having no overt political objectives except guarding and if possible expanding the role of Islam in the state. It took whatever steps were necessary in the political arena to advance its religious objectives. The NU drew most of its support from the ethnically Javanese areas of Central and East Java, and in particular from rural dwellers and landlords. A particularly important element of its constituency consisted of rural Islamic teachers called *kyai,* people who in many districts wielded very great political as well as religious influence. But the NU had little support outside its Javanese heartland.

The other two Islamic parties, PSII and Pergerakan Tarbijah Islamijah (Perti), were also traditionalist in orientation, but were strongest outside Java, the PSII in Sulawesi and the Perti in Sumatra.

None of these parties openly called for the formal transformation of Indonesia into an Islamic state, although some party members had sympathy for the Darul Islam movement led by Kartosoewirjo.

The Christian parties, Partai Katolik and Parkindo, were powerful in those regions where Christianity was the dominant religion, such as northern Sumatra and parts of eastern Indonesia. But they were, as Feith notes, 'permanent minority parties'.[9] They could be assured of their continued representation in parliament, given the solidity of their constituencies, but they could not hope ever to form government at the national level: the most they could hope to do was to participate in governments dominated by other parties. And indeed this was often the case, a tribute in part to the importance of not omitting this significant minority from political decision-making, but also to the political skills and intellectual strengths of many Christian political leaders.

Socialism

The post-war PKI was founded in October 1945, though it could trace its organisational and ideological roots back to the formation of the Indies Social Democratic Association (ISDV) in 1914. In

9. Feith H 1962 *The Decline of Constitutional Democracy in Indonesia* (Cornell University Press, Ithaca), p. 145.

1948 the party had been involved in the anti-Republican rising at Madiun in East Java. The rising was quickly defeated by troops loyal to the Republican government, and the party thrown into disarray. Many of its most prominent leaders were arrested, and some executed; branches were dissolved and members quit the party. The Republican government represented the rising, and the PKI's role in it, as a 'stab in the back', at a time when the nation was engaged in a life-and-death struggle with the Dutch.

In 1950 the PKI's organisation was weak and it had only thirteen seats in parliament. In the middle of that year, however, two young Indonesian communists, D. N. Aidit and M. H. Lukman, set about gaining control of the party, in alliance with a small group of like-minded men, the most prominent of whom were Sudisman and Njoto. By January 1951 the new guard had succeeded in wresting control of the party from the old.

Under Aidit's leadership in the early 1950s the party built up the mass base which it had previously lacked. A variety of tactics was adopted. These included consolidating the party's influence in the trade union movement, and strengthening its position in the countryside by offering to peasants services such as cheap loans, agricultural implements and seeds. But probably the most important tactic the party adopted was promoting the formation of a united national front including the petty bourgeoisie and the national bourgeoisie, albeit under the leadership of the proletariat. The breadth of this national front reflected the party's view that the 1945–49 revolution had succeeded only in securing recognition of Indonesia's political independence; it had not freed Indonesia from the economic colonialism represented by the continuing dominance of the economy by non-indigenous capital, both Chinese and European; nor had it done anything to break the power of the traditional, feudal elites in Indonesian society. Thus, despite the country's political independence, members of the petty and national bourgeoisie still suffered from oppression and exploitation, just as they had done in colonial times. The party aimed to tackle both of these aspects of the revolution left unfinished in 1949, its stated aim being: '[to] create a state which was independent, democratic, prosperous and advanced, to replace the government of the feudal bosses and compradors and to create a . . . Democratic People's government'.[10]

10. PKI Constitution, General Programme, in Kementerian Penerangan 1954 *Kepartaian dan Parlementaria*, pp. 492–3.

Despite this rhetoric of class struggle, the PKI under Aidit rejected armed revolution as the path to victory and chose instead to work through the legitimate political processes of the day, including both parliament and elections. It also adopted an accommodating line towards the role of religion in society. It was never strongly oriented towards the international communist movement nor subordinate to Moscow (or later Beijing); it was thus a very *Indonesian* communist party.

The party drew its support from a variety of sources, reflecting the range of interests it represented. It was certainly the dominant party active in the trade union movement, and had at least the passive support of many of the peasant farmers of Central and East Java. It was also well-organised among workers on the estates, plantations and mines of Java and Sumatra. It may also have had a fair degree of support from the ethnic Chinese community, though the extent of this support, as well as its depth, are open to question. Certainly the PKI was prepared to speak out publicly in defence of the Chinese as an ethnic group, something most parties were not prepared to do, and it numbered several Indonesian Chinese among its early leaders. The one group that the PKI never succeeded in penetrating to any significant extent was the intellectuals. Few people with university degrees, and almost no university students, seem to have been attracted to the party.

The major socialist, non-communist party was the Socialist Party of Indonesia, the PSI, headed by Sutan Sjahrir and formed in 1947. Its members saw themselves as Marxists, but they saw Marxism, in Sjahrir's words, not as: 'a political credo or panacea, but as one of the tools for the solution of the many problems which the party faced within the framework of the realities of Indonesian society'.[11]

The party operated in the same kind of ideological mould as Western European social-democratic or labour parties. Sjahrir insisted, however, that socialism in Asia in general, and in Indonesia in particular, was different in a number of important ways from socialism in Europe. In particular, the transfer of property rights over the means of production from the individual to the community should not be the major goal of Indonesian socialists; their attention should not be focused primarily on control over property rights but with increasing the means of production in

11. As cited in Mintz J S 1965 *Mohammed, Marx and Marhaen. The Roots of Indonesian Socialism* (Praeger, London), p. 135.

the society in such a way that overall levels of welfare could be raised.

The PSI was very much an urban-based party, and a party of Western-educated intellectuals. It was also a very selective party in membership, preferring to attract a small number of well-qualified, well-educated and well-motivated cadres, rather than a larger number of members many of whom would have had only a vague grasp of the party's ideology. In 1950 the party could claim a total membership of a few thousand; in 1952 membership stood at 3,000 full members and a little over 14,000 candidate members. By 1955 it had around 50,000 members of both kinds. Sjahrir, as leader of the party, was in many ways typical of its membership. Well-educated in the formal, Western tradition, he was a thinker and a planner rather than a populist leader. From his early days in the nationalist movement, he had urged the development of an intellectual and political elite for the country which could take over its management from the Dutch. But like the PSI itself, he found it difficult to adapt to the changing political environment of independent Indonesia, and was effectively bypassed by leaders such as Sukarno who could appeal directly to the people at large in ways Sjahrir never could. During the late 1950s Sjahrir's commitment to a basically Western style of political system came into increasing conflict with Sukarno's vision for a political order based on indigenous traditions. Having been detained by the Dutch in the 1930s, Sjahrir ended as a political prisoner of the Sukarno government and died on medical release in 1966.

Nationalism

All the political parties were nationalist in a broad sense, but only some of them declared nationalism to be their central ideological principle. The most important of these was the PNI, formed in 1946. Sukarno had no formal connection with the PNI, but his name was widely associated with it: not surprising, of course, in light of the fact that he had been closely associated with the two previous parties bearing the same name.[12]

The PNI was primarily a party of the Javanese, drawing its support from two major constituencies, one urban the other

12. The first PNI was formed in July 1927 and dissolved in April 1931; the second was the ill-fated state party which was established, and collapsed, in August 1945.

rural. Outside Java, the party had only pockets of support, chiefly in non-Muslim areas such as Bali. The urban constituency consisted largely of civil servants and white-collar employees of private enterprise: people, generally, with relatively good levels of education by the standards of the place and time, and often people from the lesser nobility. It drew little support from entrepreneurs or business people: it was a party of salary-earners rather than property-owners. Its rural constituency – like the urban one, primarily Java-based – consisted of farmers, and their families, chiefly people for whom Islam was not a major feature of daily life.

The PNI's ideological base is difficult to define in precise terms. During the independence struggle from 1945–49, it made much of standing for high-sounding but nonetheless loosely-defined principles such as 'independence' and 'nationalism'. This was no great problem for the party during the 1940s, when, for the most part, the achievement of independence was a sufficient basis on which for parties to operate. Certainly notions of ideological precision and consistency were for the most part unimportant.

After the recognition of independence, however, the party tried to evolve these vague ideas into a more adequate ideology: the revolution was over, and with it had gone the party's central focus. The party termed the ideology it eventually espoused *marhaenism*. The term very deliberately evoked memories of Sukarno, who had first popularised the term *marhaen* in the late 1920s. Sukarno used the word to refer to the ordinary poor Indonesian for whom, in his view, the word 'proletarian' was inappropriate. The term 'proletarian' implied someone who owned none of the means of production, and had only his or her labour power to sell. But *marhaen*, in Sukarno's view, did not fit this pattern because the ordinary poor Indonesian usually did own some means of production: farm implements such as a hoe or a plough; draught animals such as oxen or buffalo; tools for making goods for sale, such as a hammer or a saw; and so forth. A *marhaen* was thus rather different from a proletarian.

But when the PNI spoke of support for *marhaenism*, what exactly did it mean? Party documents from the early 1950s tend to speak of the goal of *marhaenism* in terms of the creation of a happy and prosperous Indonesian society, all members of which were treated equally without regard to religion, race or other individual characteristic; the struggle to create this society was a socio-nationalist and socio-democratic one. This is all very unexceptional; most if not all parties of the time would have been able to subscribe to most of these objectives, and with its emphasis on social justice and its religious neutrality *marhaenism* had its closest affinities with the socialist parties. But going much deeper than this is not easy. It can be said, though, that the party was nationalistic, and occasionally xenophobic, and protective of what it saw as indigenous political values and cultures. It was also in many respects an ironically conservative party. It was certainly opposed to colonialism, but it did not call for thoroughgoing change in indigenous society. In fact the reverse: it lauded traditional values and attitudes, and harked back to them as the true base to which Indonesia and Indonesians ought to return. This was a major reason for its acquiring the support of those older people who made up the vast bulk of the civil service corps, anxious to find an alternative to the Dutch values to which they had previously been tied and which were clearly inappropriate in the revolutionary environment.

Two other parties in parliament also represented this large cultural group. The PIR was a party of conservative Javanese bureaucrats keen to reaffirm the traditional values of Javanese aristocratic society, while the Partai Rakjat Nasional (National People's Party, PRN) was a former faction of the PNI which found *marhaenism* too radical for its taste. The Democratic Fraction also fell largely into this category.

THE FLOW OF POLITICS

In practical politics, the alignment of the parties did not always follow their ideological bases. This was partly because parties which were close ideologically often competed over the same following and thus distrusted each other. It was also because attitudes to issues such as modernity and social reform cut across ideological boundaries.[13] The Masjumi's orientation towards modernisation and liberal democracy gave it more in common with the PSI than with its fellow Muslims in the traditionalist NU. Although the Masjumi saw nothing threatening in the PSI's socialism, it was deeply hostile to communism, which it saw as irredeemably hostile to Islam. The PSI for its part was hostile to the PNI and

---

13. In his *Decline of Constitutional Democracy in Indonesia*, Feith divides Indonesia's political leaders into 'administrators' and 'solidarity-makers'.

the PKI despite their shared socialist roots, seeing them both as dangerously populist and inclined to adopt policies for their mass appeal rather than for the good of the country. The PNI in turn suspected that the willingness of the Masjumi and the PSI to deal with the West and with Western ideas made it ready to betray national integrity. With its uneasy internal coalition of radicals and conservatives, the PNI both feared and admired the PKI for its growing ability to reach out to the peasants, but was able itself to reach out to a variety of both traditionalist and radical groups, from the conservative PIR and PRN to the Marxist Murba. The central division in practical politics during the first half of the 1950s, therefore, was between the Masjumi and PSI on one hand and the PNI and its allies on the other, with the balance of power gradually shifting from the former to the latter, though the PKI also began to emerge as a third pole of authority as the 1955 elections approached.

Simple arithmetic shows that a cabinet with the support of a majority of members of parliament would require the participation of at least four parties. Simple politics suggests that the formation of such coalitions would be difficult, and the outcomes unstable. And this is indeed what happened. Between 1950 and 1957 Indonesia was governed by no fewer than seven different cabinets, with an average life-span of about twelve months. Hatta's last cabinet took the country through the first eight months of 1950, and he was succeeded by cabinets under Natsir (seven months), Sukiman (eleven months) and Wilopo (fifteen months). Ali Sastroamidjojo then headed a cabinet which remained in office for just under two years and he returned to office for a further eleven months after an eight month cabinet under Burhanuddin Harahap. Thus a major preoccupation for each prime minister was maintaining the solidarity of the coalition on which his government rested.

The parliamentary system has been widely criticised for its instability, but the rapid turnover of cabinets was not its most important problem. Although relations between coalition partners were always uneasy, there was a good deal of continuity of ministers between cabinets; often as many as a third of the outgoing cabinet would hold portfolios in its successor. This was because the early cabinets in particular consistently included Catholic and Protestant party members and gave prominent roles to non-party politicians, people who were chosen for ministerial ranks on the basis of their professional skills and expertise rather than of their membership of a particular party or faction.

Policies, too, remained similar from cabinet to cabinet. The Natsir, Sukiman and Wilopo governments, governing from 1950 to 1953, were concerned in particular with achieving economic stability and prosperity. The preceding two decades had seen the Depression, occupation by the Japanese and the war for independence, and all three governments put the highest priority on national reconstruction, even if this meant postponing action to achieve the social goals of the independence struggle, such as distributing national wealth more equally and reducing the role played by ethnic Chinese entrepreneurs. The cabinet of PNI politician Ali Sastroamidjojo, which succeeded that of Wilopo, put considerably less emphasis on economic management and proportionately more on foreign policy. A lawyer by training, with a degree from Leiden University in the Netherlands, Ali had come to nationalist prominence in 1927, when he was tried, along with Hatta and two other Indonesian students, on charges of attempting to subvert Dutch colonial authority in the Indies. He had also been active in international student politics, representing Indonesian students at a series of anti-colonial conferences in Europe in the 1920s and 1930s. After 1949 he served for a while as ambassador to the United States before being recalled to Indonesia to take on the prime ministership. He therefore brought to the post a sensitivity to Indonesia's international position and a long-standing reputation as a radical. Nonetheless, Indonesia's economic weakness meant that he could make no real effort to bring about social and political change. The relatively long tenure in office of Ali's first cabinet, moreover, and his return to power in early 1956 also made for some degree of policy continuity.

Postponing social and political change, however, was not just a matter of priorities: it was a consequence of the political system. The arithmetic of coalition made it impossible for any party to implement its long-term goals through parliament. Although the Masjumi, for instance, played a prominent role in three cabinets, it was never able to push the country closer to becoming an Islamic state. In this respect it was no more powerful than the PKI, which was never in government. The larger parties, thus, effectively had a veto over government policy, and this meant that policy tended to become a holding operation, bereft of long-term vision.

The same inertia operated in the public service and the armed forces. Ministers tended to appoint members of their own parties to the departments they controlled, partly as a reward for service, partly to improve the chances of their instructions being carried out loyally. This meant, however, that departments dominated by different parties often had difficulty working with each other, while departments which changed ministers frequently became internally divided between successive layers of party appointees. In the armed forces, direct links between the parties and individual units were a little weaker than they had been during the struggle against the Dutch, but party sympathies remained important. Outside Java, moreover, regional military commanders often worked closely with their civilian counterparts – mainly party politicians – in administration and economic activities. These political links entrenched the power of local commanders and made military discipline weak.

All four governments from Hatta to Wilopo attempted to reduce the size of the public service and the armed forces. They wanted both to reduce the cost of maintaining large civil and military bureaucracies, and to increase the central government's control over those bureaucracies. They had a powerful and capable ally in the army chief of staff, Colonel A.H. Nasution, who had a strong vision of a trim, well-trained and tightly disciplined army, but they faced enormous resistance from the parties and regional military establishments.

The blocking power of these entrenched interests was expressed most clearly in October 1952, when an alliance of party figures and regional military commanders thwarted an ambitious plan by Nasution to cut the army's numbers from 200,000 to 100,000. Incensed by this obstruction, Nasution and his supporters attempted to bully Sukarno into dissolving parliament, using army-sponsored demonstrations in Jakarta to condemn the supposedly undemocratic, unelected parliament. Sukarno, however, refused to be intimidated and supported the opponents of the government. Nasution was suspended from his post and from active service, while the Wilopo cabinet which had backed him was humiliated.

The October 1952 affair illustrated the political strengths and weaknesses of the parliamentary system. As it was constituted, parliamentary democracy in Indonesia proved incapable of producing a clear political direction for the country. We have seen that this was a product of parliamentary arithmetic and administrative and military structures, but it was also because the political legitimacy of the parties and the parliamentary system was shaky.

The parties were hobbled, first, by the fact that they had never faced the people in general elections. The number of seats they occupied in parliament was a historical legacy of the independence struggle, not a product of popular support at election time; the status and influence which each party enjoyed in parliament, too, depended on the skills of party leaders in striking political bargains with leaders of other parties. The problem here was not simply one of determining with a degree of certainty just how many seats any particular party was entitled to; it was also a question of political legitimacy. With no electoral results to back them up, no party's leaders could legitimately claim that they had a popular mandate to promote the platforms they pursued.

More generally, the political system had not yet struck deep roots in Indonesian society. The modern institutions of the state – not only the parliament but also the courts, the bureaucracy and the armed forces – were very much the product of Western, especially colonial, influences on Indonesia and a great many Indonesians saw no inherent value in any of these political forms. It goes too far to suggest, however, as influential observers did in the 1960s and 1970s,[14] that the parliamentary system collapsed because it was inherently alien to Indonesian political culture. As later events showed, there was no perfect formula for governing Indonesia according to its own traditions, because those traditions were so diverse.

Paradoxically, the greatest strength of the system was that it delivered a political stalemate. None of the competing ideological streams could prevail, but none of them faced defeat. The only serious attempt to exclude any major political force during this era was the Sukiman cabinet's detention of 15,000 communists in August 1951 on rather flimsy charges of subversion. Sukiman, however, was chastised in parliament for his action and the detainees were released a few months later by the Wilopo cabinet. The PKI then launched a major campaign for membership to make itself less vulnerable to such attacks. After the bitter legacy of conflict during the war of independence, the parliamentary system had an important soothing effect on Indonesian politics. The deep apprehensions and suspicions which the independence struggle had produced did not disappear, of course, but the relative civility of the parliamentary system encouraged each of the political forces to imagine that it held what amounted to a

14. The most important of such arguments came in a review by Harry J. Benda of Feith's *Decline of Constitutional Democracy*, published as Benda H J 1964 'Democracy in Indonesia'. *Journal of Asian Studies* 23: 449–56.

veto on political initiatives. A major reason, therefore, for the reluctance of the early parliamentary governments to prepare for general elections was the fear that elections might upset this comfortable stalemate by giving a political mandate to one party or another.

For all this, two critical weaknesses in the parliamentary system were becoming clear. The first was corruption. The political parties' access to power quickly degenerated into an undignified and poorly concealed scramble for the spoils of office. The Ali government in particular was marred by a number of serious corruption scandals. Although some upright leaders maintained a reputation for impeccable propriety, public respect for party politicians declined rapidly during the early 1950s and with it declined the reputation of the parliamentary system.

Second, the feeling began to grow that the stalemate was preventing governments not only from imposing narrow political goals but from adopting the policies the country needed to progress. Demand for Indonesian products created by the Korean War cushioned the economic policies of the early cabinets, but by the time of the Ali cabinet the economy was already showing signs of neglect and decay, including serious inflation. Many Indonesians hoped that the coming elections would deliver a decisive result and permit more effective government. Others, however, began to toy with the idea that an alternative to the party system might deliver capable government while still preserving the balance between competing ideological forces. Intellectually this interest in an alternative to parties focused on the idea that Indonesians might be better represented in parliament by functional groups – that is according to the role they played in society as workers, peasants, women, intellectuals, youth and so on – rather than by ideologically based parties. Such groups had been represented in the KNIP during the struggle against the Dutch and continued on a small scale in the parliament of 1950–55.

In day-to-day politics, however, interest in an alternative to parties focused on the president and the army. As the proclaimer of independence and the author of the Pancasila, Sukarno retained considerable prestige, while his position as a nominally figurehead president insulated him to a large extent from the venal politicking of the parliamentary system. The army for its part was gradually becoming more confident of its own managerial ability and increasingly inclined to see itself as a guarantor for the nation, standing above the divisions of party politics in the high-minded defence of the country. Until 1955 the divisions within the army were so great and the external connections of different units with party groups so important that it is unwise to talk of the army as a single unit. In February 1955, however, 270 senior army officers from virtually every faction and interest group met in Yogyakarta to affirm military unity in the face of civilians. Division persisted, of course, but from 1955 the army acted as a unit to a much greater extent than before. It exercised this sense of purpose in June 1955 when it refused to accept the Ali government's nomination for the post of chief of staff, boycotting the unfortunate general's installation ceremony so comprehensively that a fire brigade band had to be called in to play the national anthem. Humiliated, as Wilopo had been by the October 1952 affair, the Ali cabinet was soon forced to resign.

Signs, moreover, had begun to emerge that the early 1950s would be just a breathing space in the struggle over Indonesia's identity and that even the parliamentary system could not postpone serious conflict indefinitely. The first of these signs was the accession to power of Ali Sastroamidjojo in mid 1953. The cabinet he formed was based on the PNI, PIR and NU: there were no representatives of the Masjumi, PSI or either of the Christian parties. It was the first occasion since 1947 that the Masjumi had been excluded from a governing coalition. The shift in political power away from the Masjumi which culminated in the Ali cabinet had little to do with changing numbers in parliament – as we have seen, the relative strengths of the Masjumi and the PNI changed only slightly during this period – and had even less to do with public opinion in the rest of the country. It was based rather on the PNI's growing ability to construct a broad nationalist coalition in parliament. After the initial dismantling of federalism, the governments which preceded Ali's had generally chosen not to put priority on removing the legacies of colonialism. The Dutch-owned Java Bank, the country's reserve bank and thus the institution which issued the nation's currency and held its reserves of foreign currency, was nationalised and renamed Bank Indonesia. Western New Guinea, however, remained in Dutch hands, the enormous debt to the Netherlands remained a drain on national income, and the Dutch and other Western domination of the modern sectors of the economy remained largely unchallenged. The cabinets from Hatta to Wilopo had remained inactive in this area because they feared that the economy could not stand radical disengagement from the Dutch, but it left all their governments with the taint of preserving Indonesia's colonial dependence on the West.

The early cabinets were compromised, too, by their willingness to lean towards the United States in foreign policy for a mix of ideological and pragmatic (chiefly aid-related) reasons. There had already emerged, however, a form of orthodoxy which argued that in foreign policy matters the country should seek to be active but independent: active in international affairs, but independent of the major power blocs. This orthodoxy had become deeply entrenched in the Indonesian body politic by the early 1950s; governments ignored it at their peril. Thus, for instance, when the Sukiman government concluded an arms deal with the United States which involved a commitment to participate in the defence of the 'free world' the uproar in parliament was sufficient to bring the government down: the only time in Indonesian history when a government was brought down over a foreign policy issue.

Ali, by contrast, emphasised that Indonesians should reassert their full political, economic and moral sovereignty over their territory. Economic stability and development, while certainly not unimportant, was secondary to this principle. A first priority was to try to free Indonesia from the burden of the economic clauses of the Round Table Conference agreements, especially those concerned with the public debt of the Netherlands Indies. The Dutch retaliated by trying to seize Indonesian exports passing through the Netherlands, but this only resulted in the Indonesians diverting their exports to other markets, especially in Germany. Ali also revived the principles of the earlier Benteng programme which had attempted to shore up the position of indigenous business people, as compared with Chinese entrepreneurs. He tried this through an elaborate system of licences and permits which would have been available only to indigenous business people. But this move came to little: all that really happened was the development of various ingenious – and often successful – methods of circumventing the regulations.

Ali also vigorously took up the issue of Western New Guinea. The Round Table Conference agreements had provided that this matter would be resolved within a year. It was not. As a result, it developed into a major conflict between Indonesia and the Dutch. Ali decided to internationalise the issue, by taking the Indonesian claim to the territory to the United Nations. He failed to secure the two-thirds majority necessary in the General Assembly to force the UN to take action, but he won for Indonesia an important moral victory. More than half the UN's members had supported Indonesia; the attention of the international community had been drawn to the Indonesian claim.

Under Ali, too, Indonesia began to seek a more prominent role in international affairs in general. In the early 1950s, Indonesian policy-makers had reacted to Dutch plans for a post-colonial alliance by announcing that Indonesia's foreign policy would be 'active and independent' and, although Indonesia was very much in the Western diplomatic camp under the first cabinets of the parliamentary period, it refused to make any formal commitment to the anti-communist bloc. By the mid 1950s, however, Indonesia's self-confidence as an Asian power had grown and it had become increasingly frustrated by the West's failure to put pressure on the Dutch over Western New Guinea. Meanwhile, too, a growing number of Asian and African countries had achieved independence but were by no means satisfied with a world in which the United States and the Soviet Union, with their respective allies, dominated the globe militarily and economically. Under these circumstances, the idea arose of a third bloc in world affairs, drawing together the newly independent countries, not only for mutual support but to dissipate what they saw as the destructive atmosphere of polarisation and confrontation caused by the Cold War. The origins of this movement can be traced back to the 1940s, but the idea became reality with Ali's convening of an Asia–Africa Conference in the West Java city of Bandung in April 1955, the first in a series of what are now the conferences of the Non-Aligned Movement. The Bandung Conference attracted a crowd of distinguished visitors: Nasser, Nehru, Zhou Enlai, Tito. And Ali – and of course Sukarno – was at the centre of things. The holding of the conference marked the beginning of a decade in which Indonesia was to play a prominent role in world affairs.

Ali's foreign policy successes could not sustain his cabinet indefinitely, but by the time it fell in July 1955, Indonesia was very close to its first national elections, scheduled for September 1955. The new cabinet was expected to do little more than act as caretaker until the election results showed what political directions Indonesia could expect for the rest of the decade.

CHAPTER FIVE
Burying the Party System, 1955–59

The elections which many Indonesians hoped would deliver stable, clean and effective government were finally held in September 1955. Voting took place in an atmosphere of apprehension. Indonesians had never before voted as a nation and their pride in the exercise of democracy was tempered by uncertainty as to what result the elections might present. Indonesia's voters certainly felt the weight of their responsibility and more than thirty-nine million electors cast their ballots, a turnout of over 91 per cent.[1] Proportional representation was used, and the ballot paper thus gave voters a choice between parties, not individual candidates. Each province had a separate ballot paper and a number of local parties competed only in their own provinces, but there was a single, national quota of about 147,000 for each of 257 seats in the new parliament, and surplus votes from each province were pooled at the national level to produce the final result.[2]

Indonesia's voters ranged from well-educated city-dwellers who read newspapers and who judged the parties on the basis of a close knowledge of their policies and leadership, to illiterate country people whose choice of party was heavily influenced by respected local leaders, whether these were aristocratic, administrative, religious or military. There were certainly cases of intimidation – more

1. See the description of the run-up to polling day in Feith H 1962 *The Decline of Constitutional Democracy in Indonesia* (Cornell University Press, Ithaca), pp. 428–9.
2. The electoral law provided for an additional three seats representing the province of West Irian, to be filled by nomination; in addition, the president was empowered to appoint up to nine, six and three members to represent the Chinese, European and Arab minorities respectively if fewer than these numbers from the minorities were elected from the party lists.

than 150 election officials were kidnapped or killed[3] – and a few instances of electoral fraud, but on the whole the elections proceeded with remarkable efficiency and honesty.

Eighty-three parties and individuals registered to contest the elections, but four of these dominated the results, as can be seen from the table below:

Votes and seats won by the eight largest parties, 1955[4]

	Votes	%	Seats	Seats in provisional parliament
PNI	8,434,653	22.3	57	42
Masjumi	7,903,886	20.9	57	44
NU	6,955,141	18.4	45	8
PKI	6,176,914	16.4	39	17
PSII	1,091,160	2.9	8	4
Parkindo	1,003,325	2.6	8	5
Partai Katolik	770,740	2.0	6	8
PSI	753,191	2.0	5	14

The greatest losers in the election were the conservative nationalists of the PIR and the PRN, whose representation was virtually wiped out.[5] Never high profile, despite their numbers in parliament, and lacking clear policies for the campaign, they were unable to win more than four seats between them. The PSI, too, suffered heavily, paying for its selective membership and its concentration on cadre-building with the loss of two–thirds of its seats. Most important of all, the Masjumi was also a loser.

3. Van Marle A 1956 'The First Indonesian Parliamentary Elections'. *Indonesië* 9: 257.

4. Ibid. p. 258. The Masjumi received fewer votes than the PNI but received the same number of seats. A party had to receive about 147,000 votes to win a seat, but few, if any, party tallies exactly matched the quota. After the initial allocation of seats, therefore, the parties were entitled to pool any excess votes to reach a quota for an agreed candidate. This system gave the Masjumi three more seats than its raw vote would have won.

5. The Democratic Fraction, which also belonged to this category, did not contest the elections.

Although its support made it the second largest member force in parliament, it was the party which observers had given the best chance of winning the elections outright. Having presented itself as the primary voice of Islam in a country whose population was at least 80 per cent Muslim, its failure to win more than a quarter of the votes of Muslims was seen as a major rebuff.

The communist PKI and the traditionalist Muslim NU, on the other hand, did much better than expected. When the NU split from the Masjumi in 1952, it had taken only a few of the party's representatives in the parliament, but its power base in the countryside of Java now delivered it a standing almost equal to that of the Masjumi as a political voice of Islam. The PKI's vigorous recruitment campaigns amongst workers and peasants had been expected to produce a significant vote, but the communists' emergence as the fourth largest party, with the support of one Indonesian voter in six, was a shock to many.

Superficially, the elections brought little change to the arithmetic of coalition politics. There were more parties in parliament than before the elections but a majority coalition now required at least three parties rather than four. The apparent deadlock, however, concealed a significant shift in the balance of political power. In the old parliament, the Masjumi's numbers and self-confidence as the main Muslim party had made it the logical starting point for coalition-building. In the new parliament, bereft of its PSI allies and no longer the dominant voice of Islam, the Masjumi was more isolated. The PNI, now the strongest party, moved to centre stage, while the PKI emerged as a third pole of authority in parliamentary politics. Even though the PNI could draw some satisfaction from its status as largest party and from the elimination of the PIR and other conservative rivals, it was disturbed by the extent to which the PKI had encroached upon its following in the Javanese countryside. When Ali Sastroamidjojo returned to office in early 1956 at the head of a PNI–Masjumi–NU coalition, therefore, he pointedly omitted the PKI from his cabinet. With thirty-nine seats, however, the communists were now a force in politics which could not be ignored in cabinet-forming.

REGIONAL DISCONTENT

This shift in power was clearly a shift to the Left, but it also marked a change in political geography. In the old parliament there had been relatively little sign of regional alignments: because few of the representatives had been elected, none of them had a clear regional constituency. The mixed origins of the parliament – from the original Republic of Indonesia and from the BFO states – had also contributed to an ethnic blending. Prime ministers Hatta, Natsir and Burhanuddin Harahap were all Sumatrans, and representatives from the other islands routinely held powerful posts in successive cabinets. In the 1955 elections, however, three of the large parties – the PNI, NU and PKI – drew over 85 per cent of their support primarily from the island of Java, where about two-thirds of Indonesia's population lived. The Masjumi, on the other hand, came fourth on Java, and drew nearly half its votes from the other islands, topping the poll in all but three provinces outside Java. The PNI was strong on Bali and the NU in South Kalimantan, while the PKI had some support in the provinces of North and South Sumatra, but for the most part the Java-based parties trailed well behind the Masjumi and often behind the stronger minor parties. The PKI's support outside Java was especially sparse.[6]

This polarisation coincided not only with ethnic and religious divisions but with important divisions of economic interest. Although it would be something of a caricature to represent Java as being simply the consumer of the nation's wealth and the other islands the producer of that wealth, there would nonetheless be some truth in such a picture. For most of the twentieth century, the outer islands had been the major foreign exchange earners for Indonesia, exporting agricultural products such as rubber, tobacco and palm oil, and minerals such as coal and oil. Java, although it did also export both agricultural and mineral goods, was home to the bulk of the nation's population, and thus the place with the highest demand for food and consumer goods.

In determining their economic policies, governments in Jakarta during the first half of the 1950s – especially that of Ali – had given priority to the interests of consumers, manipulating tariff policies and exchange rates so as to ensure that imports were relatively cheap. This was of greatest benefit to Java. The other side of this coin was that Indonesia's exports were relatively expensive on world markets, and thus that the returns to commodity producers – most of whom were in the outer islands – were lower than those

6. For greater detail of the election results, see Feith H 1957 *The Indonesian Elections of 1955* (Cornell University Modern Indonesia Project, Ithaca; Interim Report Series).

which they had become accustomed to earning in earlier times. With the Masjumi now weaker and more marginal in politics, many political and business figures outside Java now feared that there would be no restraint on pro-Java policies.

Many people outside Java were alarmed, moreover, by the strength of the PKI in parliament. Muslims and Christians in the outer islands, whose beliefs tended to be more orthodox than those of their Javanese co-religionists, feared that PKI influence might mean a reduction in state support for religion as well as increased opportunities for the preaching of atheism. Because the outer islands, too, were often more commercially oriented than the Javanese heartland, these regions feared not only anti-capitalist policies inspired by the PKI but also the repercussions which might flow in international trading circles from increased communist influence in Jakarta.

Ali Sastroamidjojo's PNI–Masjumi–NU coalition had appeared on the surface to offer a continuation of the stalemate of the early 1950s, but PNI dominance soon became clear. Not only the speaker of parliament but chairmen of seven of the ten parliamentary committees were PNI members. The Ali government's policies, moreover, soon confirmed many of the fears of the islands outside Java. The rupiah remained overvalued, to the disadvantage of exporters. Ali's repudiation of much of the debt to the Netherlands agreed at the Round Table negotiations – partly to assert Indonesia's national integrity, partly to pressure the Dutch over West Irian – damaged the international standing of Indonesian businessmen. And the corrupt distribution of spoils in Jakarta created deepening resentment and contempt. By 1957 a prominent PSI politician expressed a widespread feeling when he described Jakarta as like 'a fat leech sucking on the head of a fish'.[7]

The divide between Java and the outer islands was deepened in 1956 by the resignation of Muhammad Hatta from the vice-presidency. As a Sumatran, Hatta had long been seen by non-Javanese as a crucial guarantor of the political balance between Java and the rest of the nation. His resignation was not in fact greatly influenced by any conflict between Javanese and non-Javanese interests. It had more to do with his relationship with

7. Alisjahbana S T 1970 (originally published 1957) The Grievances of the Regions. In Feith H and Castles L (eds) *Indonesian Political Thinking 1945–1965* (Cornell University Press, Ithaca), p. 322.

Sukarno and his frustration at his growing inability to influence the course of national politics. The increasingly radical nationalist tenor of national politics worried him more than geopolitical considerations. But there is no doubt his resignation was keenly felt outside Java, and interpreted in the context of the regional divide.

These circumstances put the Masjumi in an unpalatable political position. Because of its isolation in the parliament, it was in no position to dictate policy, yet as a member of the Ali cabinet it was tainted by the shortcomings of the government. If, on the other hand, it were to withdraw from cabinet, it would open the way for the PKI to take part in government.[8] Nor did the Masjumi see much to hope for in the next general elections, scheduled for 1960. Not only were the demographic factors favouring the Java-based parties unlikely to change, but the December 1955 elections for members of the Constituent Assembly, which was to decide Indonesia's new constitution, showed a pronounced swing to the PNI and parties on the Left and away from the Masjumi and PSI. Under these circumstances, Masjumi leaders increasingly began to discuss the possibility of modifying the parliamentary system and returning to the arrangement of 1948–49, when Vice-President Hatta had led a cabinet which reported, but was not directly responsible, to parliament.

Constitutional rearrangements such as this had been intended for debate in the Constituent Assembly elected in December 1955. Discussions in the Assembly, however, became deadlocked over the issue of the basis of the state (*dasar negara*). At stake was the issue which had been evaded since 1945, that is: which ideology would become the fundamental, guiding ideal behind the Indonesian nation-state? The Assembly polarised between those favouring Islam and those favouring the Pancasila. The issue was of enormous importance, but the fact that neither side could attain the requisite two-thirds majority, and the fact that practical matters of constitutional structure and political organisation seemed to be subordinate to philosophical discussion, gave the proceedings an air of irrelevance and unreality.

8. If the Masjumi refused to participate in cabinet and the PNI–NU coalition wished to rule without recourse to the PKI it would have had to construct a coalition with at least five more parties – a difficult task.

SUKARNO'S INTERVENTION

. At this point, President Sukarno acted decisively to take the debate outside the Assembly. In late October 1956 he launched a savage critique of the existing system, blaming the political parties for the country's malaise: 'we are afflicted by the disease of parties which, alas, alas, makes us forever work against one another!'[9] If parties were the problem, then the solution was simple: 'Let us bury them, bury them, bury them!'[10] In his second speech two days later, he indicated that he had a proposal – he called it his *konsepsi*, his 'concept' – about what kind of political system should replace the one then in existence, but said that he would only put it forward 'if I am asked'.[11]

Sukarno's political education and training had been Indonesian rather than European, in contrast to most of the nation's political leaders up to this time. He had never been particularly attached to the idea of liberal or parliamentary democracy, believing that Indonesians ought to seek their own form of government by looking back to their pre-colonial past, rather than by borrowing from the political conventions of the West, and in particular of the Netherlands, the former colonial power. He saw the parliamentary system as inherently divisive, causing people to direct their political energies against each other rather than towards the achievement of national political and social goals. He also looked back to what he called the Revolution, the armed struggle against the Dutch in the 1940s, which he saw as having represented the high point in political achievement for Indonesia. Though the Republic had experienced dissent, even civil war, the country had been united in the common cause against the Dutch. No such unity of purpose existed in the mid to late 1950s.

Sukarno's intervention was cryptic. His criticism of the parties did not constitute a political manifesto; rather, he was opening wider the debate on what political form might best suit Indonesia, and he was signalling for the first time that he himself was prepared to take a role in pushing that debate through to a conclusion. Just when the Constituent Assembly seemed destined to preserve the comfortable stalemate of the early 1950s, Sukarno

---

9. As translated in Feith H and Castles L (eds) 1970 *Indonesian Political Thinking*, p. 81.
10. Ibid., p. 83.
11. Ibid.

had abruptly opened the door to a still unfathomed range of possibilities. With Indonesia's future suddenly up for grabs once more, the country's political forces felt a new imperative to stake out their claims in whatever might be the new system.

The first such claim came from regional military leaders. As outer islanders, these commanders shared the dismay of the Masjumi at the pro-Java policies of the central government. They were prompted to act, however, by the policies of the army chief of staff, A.H. Nasution, reappointed to the post in 1955, after three years on the non-active list following his role in the October 1952 affair. Nasution was committed to strengthening the central hierarchy of the army, which had grown, if anything, weaker in his absence. The 1955 Yogyakarta meeting of senior army officers had affirmed army unity, but such collective leadership was hardly consistent with hierarchical discipline. Army budgets, moreover, had been reduced, and this had diminished the capacity of the central headquarters of the army to provide adequate funds to regional commanders. Many regional commanders – especially those outside Java – had had to resort to private business initiatives to secure sufficient funds to feed, clothe and equip their troops. Many of these private initiatives involved regional commanders in opening up their own international trade links, particularly through Singapore, often in collaboration with local civilian business people. Nasution had no aversion to business operations by the military, but he objected to the autonomy which such operations conferred on regional commanders, and he struck at the heart of the problem by launching a programme of large-scale transfers of regional commanders and senior officers.

Unwilling to defy Nasution directly and to destroy the military unity created at Yogyakarta in 1955, the regional commanders turned instead on the PNI-dominated government in Jakarta, which was backing Nasution both for the sake of strengthening the power of the centre and to recover the import and export revenues which it lost through army-sponsored smuggling. The regional commanders had some hopes initially that the Masjumi might come to their rescue and bring down the government, but the party was still politically adrift after its election defeat and lacked the confidence to move. Under these circumstances, the regional military commanders in Central Sumatra, North Sumatra and South Sumatra abruptly seized control of their regions, with the support of local civilian politicians, announcing that they no longer recognised the Ali cabinet and that they would govern without reference to Jakarta until a new cabinet was installed.

The Sumatra rebellion destroyed the Ali cabinet. Every day that the mutiny persisted further sapped the authority of the coalition and underlined its impotence. By the end of December, the Masjumi had decided that there was no point in staying on in a government which was bound to fall, though it was not until January that the party formally withdrew its ministers and a rump Ali cabinet limped on in parliament until March without facing a vote of no confidence. The crucial issue from the beginning of 1957 was what would succeed Ali.

Parliamentary arithmetic and precedent suggested two possibilities, but both appeared to offer a recipe for political chaos. The first possibility was a non-parliamentary Hatta cabinet, dominated by the Masjumi but drawing on other parties, including the PNI but not the PKI, for capable ministers. The Masjumi's withdrawal from cabinet was based partly on the hope that it would soon return to government with greater authority under some such arrangement. A Hatta cabinet, however, was unlikely to be accepted on Java, for it would have represented a direct repudiation of the recent elections. Hatta, moreover, might have had the confidence of the outer islands, but his term as prime minister during the independence struggle had cost him his standing as an impartial national figure; his opponents, including the PKI, which had not forgiven him for his role in suppressing the Madiun rising, were strong enough in 1957 to unleash a wave of strikes and civil disturbances on Java if he were to return to power.

The second possibility was a PNI–NU minority government which would depend on PKI support in parliament but which would not include communist ministers. Although entirely workable within parliament, such an arrangement would have exacerbated regional resentment and anxieties, not only for the exclusion of the Masjumi from power altogether but also because the PKI would for the first time be in a position to influence, even dictate, aspects of government policy. There was reason to doubt, too, whether the PNI and the NU could find enough capable ministers between them to run the country effectively.

Under these circumstances, Sukarno unveiled his thinking on Indonesia's future in February 1957. In place of the tinkering suggested by the Masjumi, Sukarno outlined a proposal for a complete restructuring of the political system, and a return to what he asserted were traditional Indonesian values. He held up the example of traditional village life in the pre-colonial era in which, he said, decisions had never been taken by vote. Rather there had been a process of exhaustive discussion (*musyawarah*) involving all members of the community, which led eventually to a communal consensus (*mufakat*) embodying not the will of a tyrannical majority of 50 per cent plus one but the interests of the community as a whole. Parliamentary politics, he said, with its culture of conflict and competition was alien to Indonesia, and its imposition in 1950 had been a parting blow from outgoing colonialism to the Indonesian national identity. For independent Indonesia, Sukarno envisaged a parliament which drew from all sections of society and which would never rely on a vote but which would aim instead for consensus.

Sukarno made two specific proposals to give effect, at least in part, to his ideas. First, he called for the establishment of a National Council, to be responsible for setting the broad outlines of national policy. The Council was to be a non-party assembly. Its membership was to be based on what were termed 'functional groups' in Indonesian society; these included farmers, labourers, women, artists, the military, students and so forth. The National Council was to parallel, at the national level, the village assembly at the local level. Sukarno himself was to be the leader of the National Council: thus his role was to be akin to that of the village head.

Second, he called for the establishment of a cabinet in which representatives of all the major political parties could hold office, irrespective of their following in the parliament. The fact that a party had a large following in the parliament would not guarantee it seats in the cabinet; nor would few seats prevent membership. And since the president himself would choose the members of the cabinet, there would be no question of one party or group of parties getting together to blackball another party – as had happened in turn to the PNI, the PSI, the Masjumi and the PKI which had all been denied cabinet posts at one time or other despite their strength in parliament. The cabinet would be responsible for the day-to-day political decisions necessary to run the country under the general direction of the guidelines set out by the National Council.

There is little doubt that Sukarno expected his *konsepsi* to be greeted widely as a gesture of national reconciliation, a break-through which would restore unity to a badly divided nation. He was disappointed. Because it made political space for the PKI while

77

leaving no room for Hatta, the *konsepsi* inevitably appeared to be favouring the communists over the Masjumi. The PKI's relatively enthusiastic reaction to the *konsepsi* strengthened this appearance. Instead of soothing tensions, Sukarno's pronouncements exacerbated them, and the regional rebellion spread.

REGIONAL REBELLION

On 2 March 1957 the regional military commander of East Indonesia, Colonel Sumual, proclaimed martial law over the whole of the territory under his command and, with other dissident military and civilian leaders adopted what they called the Charter of Universal Struggle, or Permesta. This charter called for a thoroughgoing restoration of the rights of the regions, to give them financial autonomy, a larger share of development funds and Japanese war reparations, and some control over the appointment of government officials. The National Council would only be acceptable if it became a kind of upper house or senate, protecting the interests of the regions. The charter stressed that its adherents did not wish to break away from the Republic of Indonesia, but rather to see the Republic reformed: to see it return to, and complete the implementation of, the ideals of the 1945 Revolution.

This deepening of the crisis, paradoxically, gave Sukarno the opportunity to refine his *konsepsi*. When the Ali cabinet, bereft of authority and credibility, finally resigned on 14 March 1957, Sukarno appointed what he called a Business Cabinet with the rather conservative veteran non-party politician Djuanda Kartawidjaja as prime minister. Constitutionally the Djuanda cabinet was much like a Hatta cabinet might have been: it reported, but was not responsible, to parliament, and it contained a high proportion of capable non-party politicians. It included a number of known leftists but no members of the PKI, and it also contained two members of the Masjumi, although both were expelled from their party for accepting these posts. The cabinet did not satisfy everyone, but it was a reassurance to those who feared that what Sukarno was coming to call 'Guided Democracy' would mean an abrupt lurch to the Left.

More important, the regional rebellion cemented an alliance between Sukarno and the army commander, General Nasution. As soon as the mutinies began, Nasution's aim had been to end them with as little damage as possible either to the fabric and morale of the armed forces or to the principle of military hierarchy. On the day the Ali cabinet resigned, therefore, he persuaded Sukarno to declare a State of War and Siege over the whole country, effectively declaring martial law. By retrospectively legitimising the regional military seizures of power, Sukarno and Nasution hoped to open the way for a negotiated reconciliation with the rebels. Martial law represented another step away from parliamentary democracy and from the Masjumi's hope for a Hatta cabinet, but it was immensely reassuring to conservatives because the involvement of the army in Guided Democracy appeared to guarantee that the new system would not simply become the vehicle for a communist takeover.

The place of the army in Guided Democracy was legitimate in terms of Sukarno's emphasis on the role of functional groups, but it was reinforced in different ways by three factors. First, in June–August 1957, fears of communist resurgence were confirmed when the PKI dramatically increased its share of the vote in provincial elections on Java, topping the poll in Central Java and coming second in East Java and West Java, with 27.4 per cent of the vote across the island. Conservative hopes that the PKI could be controlled within a system of parliamentary voting were dashed; if this vote were to be repeated in the general elections scheduled for 1959 then the PKI was guaranteed a role in government. Second, in December 1957 PKI and PNI trade unions seized control of Dutch-owned enterprises in Indonesia in protest against Dutch intransigence over New Guinea. The action raised the prospect of communist worker control of important industries, and the army responded rapidly by stopping further seizures and by themselves confiscating the seized enterprises and placing them under military management. The army's willingness and ability to step in and halt communist expansion was thus proven. And third, in November 1958 Nasution articulated what came to be known as the 'Middle Way' doctrine of military involvement in politics, which maintained that the army, as defender of the nation, had a duty to be involved in, though not to dominate, national politics, so as to ensure that civilian governments ruled in the national interest. Those who feared that military intervention in politics might mean no place for civilian politicians were thus partially appeased. In this way the army, although avowedly non-ideological, became a junior partner in Guided Democracy as a counter-balance to the Left.

Having accepted this position, the army moved quickly to broaden its political base by establishing what were called 'Cooperative Bodies' (Badan Kerja Sama) with the aim of detaching from the declining conservative parties their affiliated peasant, worker, youth, women's and other organisations. This was important not only to protect the army from accusations of undemocratic behaviour but to give the army a broader influence in the National Council, which Sukarno formed in May 1957. The military was only one functional group amongst many in the National Council, but by influencing the leadership of other functional groups it could create for itself a significant block of support in the assembly.

Nasution's alignment with Sukarno was not enough to reconcile the dissidents, but it was sufficient to undercut the rebel position. With hopes of a Hatta cabinet receding, a group of Masjumi and PSI politicians, together with dissident army officers, declared the Revolutionary Government of the Republic of Indonesia (Pemerintah Revolusioner Republik Indonesia, PRRI) in the West Sumatra town of Bukit Tinggi in February 1958. This was something of a desperate move, designed to galvanise the opposition to Sukarno before it evaporated, and it would have been less significant had it not received considerable covert support, particularly by way of weapons and equipment, from the United States, Britain and Australia.[12] These countries were sympathetic to the kind of anti-communism voiced by the outer islanders; their dislike of the central government had been exacerbated by Jakarta's acquiescence in the seizures of Dutch enterprises in 1957, which amounted, in their eyes, to nationalisation without compensation.

Although the PRRI in Sumatra soon made common cause with the Permesta rebels in eastern Indonesia, the central authorities crushed the uprising quickly and with relatively little violence, the affair being described at the time as an 'unnaturally civil war'.[13] This was a measure, of course, of the extent to which

12. The rebels also received support in the form of foreign personnel. Aircraft crewed by Americans, and flying from American bases in the Philippines, undertook a number of bombing raids on targets in eastern Indonesia in support of the PRRI–Permesta forces. One of these aircraft, piloted by Alan Pope, was shot down over Ambon on 18 May 1958.

13. Grant B 1967 *Indonesia* (Penguin, Harmondsworth), p. 38. According to official figures over 30,000 troops were killed in the fighting, so the civility of the struggle should not be overstated. See Penders C L M and Sundhaussen U 1985 *Abdul Haris Nasution. A Political Biography* (University of Queensland Press, St Lucia), p. 125.

the apprehensions of the rebels had been allayed by the army's participation in Guided Democracy.

Sukarno's *konsepsi* thus prevailed. With Nasution's assistance, he offered the Indonesian people not only a return to political stability but a restoration of the ideological stalemate which early parliamentary democracy had delivered. Instead of a broad coalition made on the floor of parliament, Sukarno offered an even broader coalition made in the reception halls of the presidential palace, with the PKI and the army as twin guarantors that no single vision of the future of Indonesia would prevail. It was to be a brief respite in the struggle.

CHAPTER SIX

Towards Cataclysm, 1959–65

Guided Democracy came into being with the promise of preserving the ideological standoff which had ruled in Indonesia under the parliamentary system. Although Sukarno spoke scathingly of the mendacity of the parties, he accepted all the ideologies they represented as legitimate. As he carefully unveiled his ideas for Indonesia's future, the president seemed to be describing a system in which the power of veto by all groups would be preserved. Taken at face value, such a system was unlikely ever to lead to radical change. If no majority were to be permitted to have its way, and if even small minorities were entitled to have their views incorporated into the eventual decision, then Guided Democracy offered a moderately attractive prospect of ideological stalemate as before, but without the ideological acrimony. In his series of reforms from 1957 to 1959, however, Sukarno did away with the checks and balances which had enabled the politics of stalemate to flourish, and put into place institutions which would enable him to shape Indonesia according to his own visions. Sukarno's Guided Democracy became Indonesia's first attempt to decide the complex question of national identity by executive fiat from the centre.

SUKARNO'S VISION

As Guided Democracy began to take shape, it became increasingly clear how much the parties had lost. On 5 July 1959 Sukarno took the final step in establishing his new order by dissolving the Constituent Assembly which had laboured fruitlessly for three and a half years in the drafting of a new constitution. In a triumphal gesture Sukarno then reintroduced the 1945 Constitution which had been adopted at the time of independence but discarded in the course of the independence struggle. The gesture was triumphal, both because it symbolised Sukarno's conviction that the politics of the 1950s had been a straying from the original clear vision of the Indonesian nationalist movement and because the 1945 Constitution gave him vast new powers. The 1945 Constitution provided for a strong executive presidency, with ministers responsible to the president not the parliament, and the president was himself empowered to regulate a wide range of matters by decree. Presidential favour replaced party patronage as the most effective route to high government office, while at lower levels martial law abruptly curtailed party influence in the bureaucracy and the regional administrations. Party loyalists were set to one side or were simply sidestepped as the new military administrators moved in. At the same time, the new interim People's Consultative Assembly (Majelis Permusyawaratan Rakyat Sementara, MPRS), installed in 1959 with presidential nominees narrowly outnumbering members of the old elected parliament, weakened the direct link between electoral support and legislative power. The capacity of the parties to dig their heels in and resist change was much reduced.

Increasingly, moreover, Sukarno emphasised his own leadership. He stressed the special role which *musyawarah* and *mufakat* (deliberation and consensus) gave to the leaders of the community, whose task was to guide the discussion and to articulate the eventual consensus and began to describe himself in increasingly extravagant terms, such as Great Leader of the Revolution and Mouthpiece of the Indonesian People. He argued that the principle of popular sovereignty which the war of independence had so deeply ingrained was better represented by a direct, almost mystical, relationship between Indonesians and their president than by any system of voting for political parties. From July 1959 to his post of president he added that of prime minister, a position previously filled by politicians elected through the parliamentary system. In 1963 the compliant national parliament elected him President-for-Life.

From this position of political dominance, then, Sukarno began to unfold his vision of the identity of modern Indonesia. Sukarno's ideology was an eclectic assemblage of doctrines whose emphases changed over time. It contained, however, three broad principles. First, Sukarno insisted that the ideological conflicts within Indonesian political life did not reflect irreconcilable antagonisms but rather represented different emphases within a common Indonesian world-view. He regarded himself as belonging to all religions and all progressive ideologies, and saw his role as one of articulating the essential unity of those beliefs. This was nothing new for Sukarno. In 1945 he had done precisely this in formulating the Pancasila; during Guided Democracy he developed the corresponding notion of NASAKOM as a national ideology. NASAKOM was an acronym formed from *nasionalisme*, *agama* (religion) and *komunisme*, and was meant to symbolise the ideological unity of the three major streams within Indonesian politics. Even NASAKOM was not entirely a product of post-war thinking: in the late 1920s and early 1930s Sukarno had been arguing for the need to unify the three major strands of the nationalist movement – Nationalism, Islam and Marxism – under his leadership.

Second, Sukarno took a largely corporatist view of Indonesian society, arguing that society was best thought of as a joint endeavour by different functional groups – workers, peasants, officials, intellectuals, soldiers, students, women – and that national goals could be achieved only when sectional interests were subordinated to the interests of the whole. Accordingly, over a third of the representatives in the MPRS were drawn from specified functional groups. Sukarno largely rejected the idea that there were significant class divisions within Indonesia; as we have seen in Chapter 4, even before the Second World War he had coined the term *marhaen* to describe the typical poor Indonesian peasant who owned a small plot of land as well as his tools and animals and for whom the Marxist term proletarian – referring to someone with nothing to sell but labour – was inappropriate. The absence of classes, he argued, precluded class exploitation in its true sense. Rather than class conflict, therefore, Sukarno argued that the *marhaen* needed compassion and sympathy from the state and from the rest of society, and he gave this doctrine of social responsibility the name *marhaenism*.[1]

Third, having denied the significance of ideological or class differences within Indonesian society, Sukarno tried to place that society in a global context, in which ideology and class – at least as between nations – certainly did have a place. He

---

1. *Marhaenism*, of course, was also the official doctrine of the PNI; as we have argued in Chapter 4, however, it was an even vaguer doctrine in the hands of party politicians than when described by Sukarno.

stressed that Indonesians needed to see themselves as being part of a great global movement of peoples united in their struggle against colonialism and oppression. Indonesia had a particular responsibility to play a major role in this movement as a former colony itself, and as a founder of the Asia–Africa and Non-Aligned Movements; anti-colonialism, moreover, had been written into the Preamble to the 1945 Constitution. The global struggle Sukarno characterised as that between what he called the Old Established Forces (Oldefos) and the New Emerging Forces (Nefos). The former were represented chiefly by governments such as those in the United States and Britain and by international capital; the latter by the liberation and anti-colonial movements as epitomised by the governments of the newly-independent states and the states of Eastern Europe, and by progressive forces within the colonial world such as trade unions and civil rights movements. Representing these states, he said, Sukarno made a major speech before the United Nations in 1960 which he titled 'Building the World Anew'. His basic argument was that for the first time in modern history the colonialist countries were outnumbered on the global stage by the anti-colonialist countries – amongst whose number he included the communist states of Eastern Europe. As a result, a new world order could be created, and a new United Nations, which reflected this shift in the balance of power; and in this process, Indonesia had a major role to play.

This struggle was a global one, but Sukarno also made it a personal one for Indonesia and Indonesians. Remembering how powerful antagonism to the Dutch had been in creating Indonesian unity in the colonial era and during the war of independence, Sukarno sought to reaffirm national unity by stressing what the alleged enmity of outside powers was costing the Indonesian people. Thus he argued that Indonesia's subordinate place in the world economy and the consequent poverty of so many of its people, despite the country's abundant natural wealth and human resources, was the result of a global imperialist order sustained by what he called the NEKOLIM (neo-colonialists, colonialists and imperialists), of whom Britain and the United States were the leaders. The nationalisation of Dutch property in 1957 had been one step towards breaking the power of the NEKOLIM in Indonesia, in Sukarno's view, but establishing a new and equitable world order required vigorous action beyond the borders of Indonesia, especially with other 'New Emerging Forces' within the non-aligned movement.

He also pointed to the continuing Dutch occupation of West New Guinea or West Irian, which all nationalists regarded as an integral part of Indonesia's territory. In late 1961, after the Dutch stepped up preparations for separate political development in the territory with the formation of a quasi-legislative New Guinea Council, Sukarno announced that Indonesia would add military measures to its campaign. The Supreme Command for the Liberation of West Irian (KOTI) was established, headed by Sukarno himself, with Nasution as his deputy, and with an operational command to carry out the liberation under a field officer, Major-General Suharto. Small-scale Indonesian military incursions into West Irian began soon after and, although these presented no immediate problem for the Dutch, they made Indonesia's determination clear and contributed to the United States' decision to pressure the Dutch to abandon the territory. On 1 October 1962, the administration of Western New Guinea was transferred to a temporary United Nations authority which in turn passed control to Indonesia in May 1963.

The most spectacular example of Indonesia's activist foreign policy, however, was the Confrontation with Malaysia from 1963 to 1965. Malaysia had been pieced together in 1963 as a federation of former British colonies and protectorates in Southeast Asia and comprised the Malay peninsula, the island of Singapore and the two northern Borneo territories of Sabah and Sarawak. Sukarno objected to the plan because he saw Malaysia as a British neo-colony, in which Britain would retain not only its extensive economic interests but also its Singapore naval base. He also objected to the continuing power of the Malay sultans, which he regarded as undemocratic, and to the fact that the federation was being imposed in the face of what seemed to be hostile public opinion in the Borneo territories. Underlying these objections was also a sense of pique that Indonesia, the largest country in the region, had not been consulted at all by Britain in its planning. Although Confrontation never reached the level of full-scale war, Indonesia made armed incursions into both East and West Malaysia, and when Malaysia became a temporary member of the United Nations Security Council in January 1965 Indonesia left the UN and began moves to organise an alternative Conference of the New Emerging Forces (CONEFO).

Sukarno made foreign policy as if Indonesia were a great power, but the reality was that the country had little power to project beyond its own borders. None of Indonesia's Asia–Africa bloc associates joined it in leaving the United Nations, and the incident marks the start of a long period of diminished Indonesian influence in the Non-Aligned Movement. The incursions into Malaysia, too, were easily defeated by British, Australian and New Zealand forces and Indonesian hostility cemented the Malaysian national identity rather than undermining it. Nor was Indonesia in a position to be truly independent in world affairs. After deteriorating relations with the United States led to a reduction in the previously strong military contacts, Indonesia turned to the Soviet Union, incurring a massive debt for Soviet military equipment. By early 1965, Indonesia had moved away from the Soviet Union and closer to the People's Republic of China. Sukarno began to talk of a 'Jakarta–Peking [Beijing] Axis' (which was sometimes extended to include Pyongyang, Hanoi and Prince Sihanouk's Phnom Penh), while opening arms negotiations with the Chinese.

POLITICAL RESTRICTION AND ECONOMIC DECLINE

For a country deeply disappointed with the fruits of independence, however, Sukarno's ideologising and activist foreign policy had a powerful appeal. Sukarno himself was a magnificent orator, able to hold the attention of vast crowds for hours at a time. The attention which Indonesia increasingly commanded in international circles was also a source of pride for many Indonesians. But more important, he restored to Indonesian politics a sense of national agenda which he described as a return to the revolution. Many countries which go through renewal by armed revolution suffer a sense of anti-climax and disappointment when the hopes and moral certainties of revolutionary struggle founder on the tedium of day-to-day administration, the venom of political antagonisms and the intractability of social and economic problems. Sukarno's reaffirmation of the revolution put a sense of dynamism and shared purpose back into national political life. Sukarno restored excitement and anticipation to Indonesian politics with freshly-coined terms such as TAVIP (The Year of Living Dangerously) and Berdikari (Standing on One's Own Feet). Even Indonesians who disliked Sukarno's personality and rejected his philosophical position applauded the unifying effect of his return to national politics.

The extent of public support for Sukarnoism, however, is made hard to judge by the fact that it soon took on the character of a required political orthodoxy. Sukarno's claim that NASAKOM combined and superseded nationalism, religion and communism could never have been expected to convince even a small minority of the adherents to those beliefs and, even though most politically minded Indonesians preferred Sukarnoism to the victory of their opponents, unqualified loyalty to Sukarno's ideas was limited to a small sincere circle. In public debate, however, hesitancy and qualification were not permitted: throughout the early 1960s, political discourse had to be undertaken within the idiom of Sukarnoism. Figures from the communist party, from the conservative Muslim Nahdatul Ulama and from the military could all be heard speaking with similar vocabulary, each group trying to squeeze its own preferred message from the body of Sukarnoist doctrine. For all its public appearances of success in unifying the Indonesian people, however, Sukarno's corporate ideology did little more than paper over the country's deepening social and ideological divisions. And while active participation in the great global movement against imperialism was required of all, few people saw such activity as justifying the increasingly precarious economic position they faced as the 1960s progressed.

Dutch colonialism and Japanese occupation had accustomed Indonesians to speaking circumspectly in public, but the hegemony of Sukarnoism was something new. Because it was a loose ideological garment, Sukarnoism could be shaped by the wearer to fit a wide variety of underlying principles, but the fact that Sukarno was able to enforce even public orthodoxy was a chilling portent to all Indonesians of the power which the state was acquiring to insist on what its subjects believed. In 1960, moreover, Sukarno banned the Masjumi and PSI on grounds of the participation of some of their members in the PRRI–Permesta rebellion. Other dissenters found themselves under house arrest or sent into exile abroad. Newspapers which offered heterodox views were banned. Ever since independence in 1945, Indonesians had been used to a somewhat ramshackle state whose institutions were so limited in capability and internally divided that it could act effectively only when it genuinely enjoyed the enthusiastic support of most Indonesians. Sukarno's state was never powerful enough to be totalitarian, but now, for the first time, politically-minded Indonesians of Left and Right had direct experience of the kind of measures their opponents might take on coming to power. The stakes of politics were further raised.

Sukarno's plan to reshape independent Indonesia was conceived in terms of ideology, rather than government policy. Indeed, one of the most striking features of Guided Democracy was the lack of a clear policy direction on the specifics of government. Sukarno devoted great attention to the ideological basis of the state, and was closely involved in setting in place new state institutions and in strengthening the power of the state as a whole. But he used this power to pursue very few policy innovations. Instead, he allowed himself to become the focus of attempts at influence by officials and petitioners at his court. He did not initiate policy, but he ensured that nothing could go ahead without his own approval. Sukarno's greatest practical interest was in the detail of state ceremonies and monuments. His Jakarta became studded with monuments and public buildings designed to reflect the greatness of the Indonesian nation and to inspire its people to greater efforts. This emphasis on form and ceremonial splendour, more than anything else, has led observers to compare Sukarno to the kings and sultans of pre-colonial Indonesia who accumulated power as an end in itself and poured their energies into pomp and show.[2]

Sukarno's general disregard for policy detail was most obvious in the area of economic management. Almost a decade of war in the 1940s had left much of Indonesia's productive infrastructure in ruins. Underinvestment, corruption and lack of expertise during the early 1950s had compounded the problem. Little improved after the nationalisation of foreign enterprises in 1957. There were no local funds available to recapitalise these ventures, nor many local experts to staff them. Moreover, many of the new military managers milked their firms for cash, either corruptly or to cover shortfalls in the military budget. The declining efficiency of the bureaucracy reduced the government's income and limited its capacity to assist economic growth. The high priority which Sukarno placed on the recovery of Irian and later on Confrontation led to massive defence spending which placed a further strain on the budget. The notion of a 'Guided Economy' was one of the official principles of Guided Democracy,

2. This theme in traditional Indonesian politics is discussed by Anderson B R O'G 1972 The Idea of Power in Javanese Culture. In Holt C (ed.) *Culture and Politics in Indonesia* (Cornell University Press, Ithaca and London), pp. 1–69. and Geertz C 1980 *The Theater State in Nineteenth-Century Bali* (Princeton University Press, Princeton).

but always subordinate to more 'political' principles. Sukarno maintained that the most important task in the management of the economy was political: setting the right political climate within which the economy was expected to operate. Nationally, this meant ensuring that Indonesians, not foreigners, had control of the economy and its various elements; internationally, it meant continuing the struggle against the machinations of NEKOLIM and the Oldefos. Once this political task had been achieved, attention could be turned to the details of the management of the economy. He firmly rejected the idea that economic management was something requiring purely technical skills unconnected with politics, and was particularly harsh on those who dared to disagree with him on this matter. In 1963, following the conclusion of the campaign to recover Irian Jaya, and during a brief period of good relations with the United States, Sukarno did seem to deviate from this policy, permitting the enactment of a series of regulations which represented an 'economist's' approach to management of the economy,[3] and would have made it more amenable to capitalism, both local and foreign. But the death later that year of the First Minister, Djuanda Kartawidjaja, a capable economic manager and the main proponent of these measures, effectively put paid to these regulations; thereafter the economy began to run out of control.

Ambitious international borrowing pushed Indonesia's foreign debt to US $2.1 billion by 1965. In the final year of Guided Democracy no state budget was produced. Whatever Sukarno's social and political policies may have achieved for Indonesia, his economic policies had the country in ruins by the mid 1960s, with accelerating inflation, crumbling infrastructure and an agricultural sector whose production fell increasingly short of the country's needs. Although the chaos gave economic opportunities to some, especially on the fringes of legality, the closing years of Guided Democracy were a time of increasing hardship for almost all Indonesians, comparable only to the suffering of the Depression and the Japanese occupation.

SUKARNO, THE COMMUNISTS AND THE ARMY

Public political discussion made no mention of the presidential succession, yet paradoxically this question hovered over Guided

3. Legge J D 1973 *Sukarno: A Political Biography* (Penguin, Harmondsworth), p. 332.

Democracy almost from the start. Born at the turn of the century, Sukarno was by no means an old man when Guided Democracy brought him to the pinnacle of his power, but in a society where life expectancy for males was still in the forties most people were aware that his remaining active years were likely to be few. He enjoyed the presidential lifestyle, and had become noticeably overweight and unfit. Sukarno's power, moreover, lay in his control of language and ideology, in his unique relationship with the Indonesian people, cultivated over four decades of intense political activity. In his immediate circle of loyalists, one or two – perhaps Chaerul Saleh and Ruslan Abdulgani – showed inspiration as ideologists, but no one came close to him in public appeal. Without Sukarno's magic at the centre, Guided Democracy could not survive, and there was a growing feeling, which still could not be expressed publicly, that Sukarno's departure would unleash the struggle for political hegemony which Guided Democracy had briefly smothered.

Of the ideologies which had contested the 1955 elections, only communism appeared to have progressed under Guided Democracy. This was for three reasons. First, the PKI under Aidit was the only major party which seriously attempted to maintain and develop a strong party organisation. Clearly defined administrative structures, an impressive stable of party publications for different audiences, a strong research and training programme for its cadres, and well-publicised ethos of discipline and devotion made the party a formidable organisation matched in internal coherence only by sections of the armed forces. The PKI continued its efforts to win popular support, undertaking a massive recruiting drive in the cities and countryside, which boosted its membership to a claimed three million. In every sector of society, moreover, it established affiliated mass organisations. The party's peasant wing, the Barisan Tani Indonesia (Indonesian Peasants' Front), claimed eight million members, while official membership of the party's associations for youth, women, fishermen, teachers, and so on, totalled another twelve million.

This spectacular expansion, which turned the PKI into the largest communist party in the non-communist world, was possible partly because of the party's skilful selection of issues on which to campaign. The central authorities of the party presented a general blueprint for the future of Indonesia which emphasised nationalist issues at the expense of more divisive class issues; the party was especially vocal over the Irian issue, of course, but it also publicly deplored what it saw as destructive Western cultural influences brought to Indonesia by foreign films and pop music, and played a major role in restricting the dissemination of foreign culture within Indonesia. At a regional level, on the other hand, the party took sides in a multitude of local issues across the breadth of the archipelago. Most of these issues had to do with control of land and conditions of labour – the party was especially active amongst plantation workers in East Sumatra and amongst landless peasants in Java – but the party consciously and deliberately engaged in ethnic, religious, intellectual and other conflicts throughout Indonesian society, partly to recruit support and partly to reinforce the proposition that all conflict could be interpreted in Marxist terms.

Second, the PKI adopted an unusually pragmatic attitude towards the institutions of the state. In orthodox Marxism, the state is normally regarded as a tool of the ruling class which must be dismantled and reconstructed when the ruling class is overthrown. The PKI, however, argued that the Left could seize control of the state section by section, transforming each section in turn from an 'anti-People' orientation to a 'pro-People' one. A major platform of the party during the early 1960s, therefore, was the NASAKOM-isation of government, meaning in practice the insertion of PKI members or sympathisers into political and administrative posts at every level. This was accompanied by so-called 're-tooling' campaigns intended to eliminate prominent opponents of the party from positions of power. As a result, significant sections of the state took on an increasingly leftist appearance. The Department of Agriculture, whose work brought it into direct contact with peasants and fishermen, was especially influenced by the Left; so was the teaching profession within government schools. The airforce, whose equipment and training came especially from the Soviet bloc, was also sympathetic. Even within the army, the left-wing sympathies of some units were no secret, and the party had established a special bureau (Biro Chusus) to cultivate these military connections.

The third reason for PKI success was the backing it received from Sukarno himself. Because of its large membership, the party could mobilise the masses in support of the president more effectively than any other force in the country. Because, moreover, the PKI's Marxism had abandoned violent revolution and accepted the legitimacy of the Republican state, Sukarno found relatively little in the party's public pronouncements with which he dramatically disagreed. For these things Sukarno rewarded the PKI. Throughout Guided Democracy, he publicly affirmed the party's legitimacy in the Indonesian political order; he gave it occasional protection, as in 1960 when he overruled a number of regional military commanders who had banned the party within their jurisdictions; and from time to time he removed individuals and groups whom the PKI found troublesome, even banning the Murba party, left-wing rivals of the PKI, in early 1965.

The PKI's exuberance threw the other major forces of Indonesian politics into an alliance of desperation. The anti-communist coalition drew together modernising nationalists who deplored Guided Democracy's emphasis on political correctness and Sukarno's neglect of the economy and administration, and revivalist nationalists who lamented the bitter political divisiveness of a system which had been introduced in the name of national unity. The ideological pivot of this coalition, however, was Islam. Many Muslims loathed the PKI for its atheism and feared that communist rule would change Indonesia from a state which accepted and supported all religions to one which accepted and supported none. Socially, the anti-communist coalition drew on the established forces which had most to lose from a PKI victory – landlords and larger landowners, senior bureaucrats and aristocrats, businessmen and investors – though there were exceptions in all these categories who supported the communists.

The political pivot of this coalition, however, was the army. The willingness, even eagerness, of the army, and especially its commander, General Nasution, to assume some administrative and political responsibility had been an essential element in the creation of Guided Democracy. The corporate state ideology legitimised the armed forces' participation in parliament and in politics in general, martial law gave them the means to set their stamp on the country and the campaigns for West Irian and against Malaysia emphasised their key role in promoting the national interest. Under Guided Democracy, military officers held one-third of the posts in cabinet as well as a vast array of other official positions, especially as managers of state enterprises. KOTI even came to rival the cabinet as the key decision-making body within the government.[4] The armed forces were the only section of society whose internal hierarchy and sense of discipline matched that of the PKI and

4. See Crouch H 1978 *The Army and Politics in Indonesia* (Cornell University Press, Ithaca) pp. 48, 54–5.

they were strongly aware that their political authority would be circumscribed if the PKI came to power in the aftermath of Guided Democracy.

A hint of what might be in store came in 1962, when Sukarno had Nasution promoted to the largely ceremonial post of armed forces commander, replacing him with the apparently more tractable Ahmad Yani. In 1963, moreover, Sukarno abruptly ended martial law on the grounds that the recovery of Irian had made direct military involvement in government unnecessary. The army watched this reduction in its authority with misgivings. The army's officer corps tended to be drawn from the rural and small-town elite which was largely opposed to the PKI. The army, moreover, had developed a strong professional aversion to the communist party as a result of the 1948 Madiun affair, which many officers saw as a stab in the back at a crucial point in the armed struggle against the Dutch. During 1965 the growing warmth of Indonesia's ties with China further worried the army's leaders, who feared direct Chinese backing for the PKI. The army's antagonism to organised Islam was also strong, thanks to its long and bitter struggle against the Darul Islam, but Islam presented no immediate threat in the context of Guided Democracy, and the army was willing to make whatever alliances it needed in order to fend off a PKI victory.

From early in the 1960s, therefore, Indonesians and outside observers expected a major change in Indonesian politics to accompany the departure of Sukarno, whenever that might happen. Just who would prevail, however, was entirely unclear. No one could measure the depth of commitment which the PKI's three million members and twenty million affiliates in the mass organisations felt towards the party and its goals; the party often recruited people to train them as Marxists, rather than accepting only the fully committed. No one could measure the extent of implacable hostility to the PKI amongst the Muslim community, and no one could be sure just how far the PKI's penetration of the Indonesian state had proceeded. Not only did the ideological hegemony of Sukarnoism and formulas such as NASAKOM lie like a heavy cloak over political debate, making the political order increasingly opaque to observers, but many Indonesians cultivated a deliberate ambiguity in their political stances, and sought to avoid committing themselves to one side lest the other win.

There were three signs, however, that the PKI was not poised to achieve power simply through the policies of the Aidit leadership.

First, even at the height of the party's influence under Guided Democracy, only one communist minister was in charge of a government department. However striking the PKI's penetration of the bureaucracy might have been, it was still far from the point where significant sections of the administration might be described as communist-dominated. Second, the party effectively acknowledged the slenderness of its support within the armed forces in late 1964 by beginning to press for the creation of a 'Fifth Force' of armed workers and peasants, alongside the four regular armed forces (army, navy, airforce and police). Ostensibly this force was to be used in Indonesia's Confrontation with Malaysia, but it was a clear challenge to the existing armed forces' monopoly of weaponry and a tacit admission by the PKI that decisive influence within the armed forces was beyond its reach.

A third reason for believing in PKI weakness was its inability to establish a significant power base in the provinces. Only two provincial governors were sympathetic to the party, but Bali's left-wing governor, Suteja, faced determined resistance from most of the island's Hindu establishment, and North Sumatra's Ulung Sitepu was pitted against powerful military interests in the nationalised plantation sector.[5] The party, moreover, was thrown clearly on to the defensive when it attempted to implement a land reform programme in East Java in late 1963. A land reform law providing for the break-up of larger holdings had been on the books since 1960, but its implementation had been thwarted by the obstructiveness of local landowners and sections of the bureaucracy. The PKI's 'unilateral actions' (*aksi sepihak*) to implement the programme in East Java often involved seizing land from larger landowners and handing it over to tenants; the campaign pitted the party against the rural elite, most often orthodox Muslims already thoroughly antagonistic to the communists. A series of violent clashes took place well into 1964 in which the landlords and their rural allies generally managed to roll back the PKI campaign, leaving the party's base amongst poor peasants intact but casting doubt on its capacity to win a struggle in the countryside.

By 1965 Indonesian politics was poised on the brink of cataclysm. As Guided Democracy staggered on, political life was suffused increasingly by hatreds. For all Sukarno's efforts to focus hostility on external foes, most Indonesians saw their bitterest enemies

5. Crouch, *Army and Politics*, pp. 77–8.

95

within Indonesia itself. As a result of the PKI's vigorous campaigning, there was hardly an issue dividing Indonesians which could not be interpreted in terms of communism and anti-communism.[6] The PKI's insistence on political correctness even in areas such as art and literature led to savage feuds, while parts of Central and East Java seemed close to civil war. The debate over national identity which had begun when the idea of Indonesia first drew a following amongst the people of the archipelago had polarised into a frightening stand-off between communism and its opponents. The Indonesian state was now more powerful than it had ever been before; whichever political force could control that state would gain a decisive advantage in imposing its will on society as a whole. For the moment, President Sukarno still held the central institutions of the state within his grasp, but everyone recognised that the moment of his departure would be crucial to the fate of the country.

6. Ironically, Indonesia's environmentalist movement traces part of its origins to a group of students who chose, metaphorically, to withdraw into the wilderness to avoid the politicisation of all other areas of life.

CHAPTER SEVEN

The Coup, the Massacres and the Fall of Sukarno, 1965–66

The hurricane which had been brewing over Indonesian politics under Guided Democracy finally broke at the beginning of October 1965. The precise course of events which followed during the next six months is shrouded in uncertainty. Many of the key players perished or were otherwise silenced; rumour, half-truth and deliberate misinformation filled the air; and the sheer chaos of the time made it impossible for anyone to follow exactly what was happening. Only the outcome is entirely clear: the PKI was eliminated as a political force, around half a million of its members and supporters were killed, and the armed forces, headed by General Suharto, emerged as the pre-eminent political force in the country.

The chain of events leading to cataclysm began in mid-1965 as rumours started to circulate that the army's most senior generals were planning a *coup d'état* against Sukarno, possibly to take place on Armed Forces Day, 5 October. There is no especial evidence that the generals had concrete plans of this kind, but the rumours seemed entirely plausible; the army had strong incentive to move before the PKI was able to begin training a 'Fifth Force', and it is hard to believe that the army – and for that matter the PKI as well – did not have at least a contingency plan ready in case Sukarno were to die suddenly. In any event, the rumours intensified when Sukarno collapsed at an official engagement on 4 August. Those who did not wish to see an army victory – the PKI, Sukarno himself and the Sukarnoists, those whose commitment to Guided Democracy was genuine and who feared the consequences of a victory by either the PKI or its opponents – were fully aware, too, that withstanding an army coup once it had been launched would be exceptionally difficult. Their thoughts turned, therefore, to forestalling any such coup.

In retrospect, one can say that the army's opponents had three options. They could hope that the atmosphere of political uncertainty which Guided Democracy had created would keep the army off balance and sufficiently unsure of itself to hesitate before risking a coup. They could take some initiative to throw the army's plans into confusion. Or they could pre-empt the projected military coup by staging one of their own. We shall never know for certain what plans the PKI and Sukarno were making during these months, but sometime in the second half of 1965 a group of Sukarnoist junior officers, including Lieutenant-Colonel Untung (commander of the Tjakrabirawa presidential palace guard), seem to have chosen the second option. The idea arose of preventing the coup by kidnapping the generals said to be planning it. During the war of independence, the kidnapping of conservative political figures in order to jolt them into a more radical stand had often occurred and the kidnapped figures were normally released unharmed, their self-confidence shaken, their prestige undermined and their ability to act decisively therefore reduced.

It is probable that this is what a number of squads of Tjakrabirawa soldiers had in mind when they arrived at the Jakarta homes of seven senior generals, including Nasution and Yani, very early on the morning of 1 October 1965 and told the officers that they had been summoned to the palace for a meeting with the president. Much had changed in Indonesian politics, however, since the idealistic days of 1945. Called unexpectedly from their beds, the generals were immediately suspicious. They sensed personal danger and they resented the affront which the early rousing seemed to imply. They refused to obey the summons. The would-be kidnappers were thus faced with two choices. They could back off, return empty-handed to their barracks and rely on Sukarno's support to ensure that they were seen simply as exuberant revolutionaries, not mutineers. Or they could carry on with their plans, using force if necessary to capture the generals. We will never know for certain how individual soldiers made their choices; however, the leaders of all seven groups ultimately took the second option and pressed on, prepared to use force. In the ensuing mêlées, three generals, including Yani, were shot or bayoneted, and another three were captured. Nasution narrowly escaped by leaping his garden wall and seeking safety in the grounds of the neighbouring Iraqi Embassy, but his adjutant was carried off in his place. The Tjakrabirawa troops then took the living and the dead to Halim airforce base, southeast of Jakarta.

The murder of three generals, including the army commander, suddenly changed the complexion of the whole affair. The killings of Yani and his colleagues were the first political assassinations since the executions of Amir Sjarifuddin and Tan Malaka during the war of independence,[1] and the army's sense of corporate solidarity ensured that such a crime would not go unavenged. The only way forward for Untung and his colleagues therefore was to move from the limited kidnapping operation to a full-scale pre-emptive coup. As dawn broke on the morning of 1 October, the remaining generals, together with Nasution's adjutant, were hastily killed and their bodies dumped in a well at Halim. Then, at 7.00 a.m. Untung had an announcement broadcast over state radio, stating that a '30 September Movement' under his command had arrested senior generals who were plotting a coup and that Revolutionary Councils would soon be established in Jakarta and the provinces to carry out Sukarno's policies and to maintain the integrity of Guided Democracy. A second broadcast four hours later declared that the promised central Revolutionary Council had taken over 'all power' prior to new elections.

One of the great unresolved questions around these events is the extent to which other forces may have been behind Untung and his colleagues in planning the kidnappings and in escalating the operation to a full-scale coup. Sukarno, of course, might have been expected to have had special influence with the commander of his own palace guard, while the PKI's Special Bureau, responsible for cultivating party contacts within the armed forces was almost certainly in contact with some of the key figures around Untung. If we accept that the kidnapping and humiliation of the generals was the original purpose of the plot, then both Sukarno and the PKI may well have been involved. Their complicity is suggested by the fact that Sukarno and the PKI leader Aidit were present at Halim airforce base at the time of the kidnappings. The statements of PKI exiles, as well as the far more suspect testimony of PKI defendants at later trials, also indicate that sections of the PKI were in league with the Untung group in planning the affair.[2]

1. Sukarno had been subject to at least three attempted assassinations, one of which – a grenade attack made in November 1957 while he was picking his children up from school in Jakarta – caused several deaths amongst his staff and bystanders.

2. See Mortimer R 1968 'Indonesia: Emigré Post Mortems on the PKI'. *Australian Outlook* 22: 347.

PKI involvement in the Untung plot is further suggested by the fact that there is no indication at all of other plans by the party to forestall the projected generals' coup which most people expected, after all, a few days later.

The Suharto government asserts the PKI's guilt with absolute conviction, arguing not only that the party was involved but that it masterminded the whole affair. The legitimacy of the military government's accession to power, and of the anti-communist pogrom which accompanied it, is based on this interpretation of events. It also believes that Sukarno was deeply involved in the PKI plot, though it has been reluctant to press this point hard, testimony perhaps to the depth of Sukarno's popular appeal, even up to the present day.

There is little evidence or reason, however, to support the proposition that the killing of the generals or the subsequent attempt at a full-scale *coup d'état* was specifically planned by either the PKI or Sukarno. The evidence against Sukarno amounts to little more than his presence at Halim. In the immediate past, his standard response to crises had been creative inactivity: there is no strong reason to suppose that he would have broken this habit to join the planning, although the planners must have expected that the kidnappings would enjoy the president's approval.

Some PKI leaders were at the Halim base (though many others were not); and the main PKI newspaper, *Harian Rakjat*, continued to denounce the dead generals. But whereas the PKI had built up for itself a reputation for efficient planning and organisation, Untung's supposed coup bore the hallmarks of an affair lacking in preparation, planning and direction. Untung's central Revolutionary Council was a concoction of names of political figures, most of whom had not been consulted, and his only formal policy decision as chairman of the council was a hamfisted attempt to win wider support by abolishing all military ranks above lieutenant-colonel and promising promotions to all privates and non-commissioned officers who supported the coup. Moreover, although troops supporting Untung had captured the state radio station and the telecommunications centre in the heart of Jakarta early on 1 October, the rebels remained strikingly inactive during the rest of the day, as if they had no clear idea of how to proceed with seizing power. Nor did they succeed in rallying support elsewhere in the country, except in Central Java where several infantry units declared for the coup and local Revolutionary Councils were formed in a few towns.

This inactivity cost Untung the initiative and soon formidable forces began to assemble to crush him. Leader of the counter-coup forces was Major-General Suharto, commander of the army's strategic reserve, KOSTRAD, and the most senior general not on the kidnappers' list. Suharto's absence from this list has given rise to a good deal of speculation about links which he himself may have had with the plotters.[3] Although a number of questions remain unresolved, he was probably spared simply because he was not a member of the Yani group and because he was regarded as one of those generals who would adapt themselves to whatever political order might be in place. These perceptions proved to be mistaken, for Suharto moved rapidly during the hours after the coup attempt was announced. By the afternoon of 1 October he had gained control of the radio station and other buildings in central Jakarta, and by early evening he had issued an ultimatum to the groups at Halim which led Untung, Sukarno, Aidit and other leaders to abandon the airbase. By dawn on 2 October, the 30 September Movement had been defeated.

Although the coup had been suppressed, however, it was not immediately clear just what had changed in Indonesian politics. Sukarno, in particular, seemed determined to carry on as before, describing the death of the generals as a 'ripple in the ocean of the Revolution',[4] declining to attend their funeral and appointing as Yani's replacement Major-General Pranoto, who was widely known as sympathetic to NASAKOM. For a moment it seemed as if Guided Democracy might stagger on almost as before. Under these circumstances, Suharto and the senior officers around him decided to embark on a comprehensive restructuring of Indonesian politics to eliminate forever what they saw as the communist threat. The coup's failure provided the perfect pretext for the event it had aimed to forestall: a seizure of power by the army.

As a relatively little-known general, however, Suharto did not suppose that he could seize power at once. His standing within the armed forces and with the Indonesian public was not significantly greater than that of Untung. Yani may possibly have hoped to

---

3. These suspicions include suggestions that Suharto and/or other sections of the army may have counter-infiltrated the PKI's Special Bureau and used it to lead the PKI into an abortive grab for power which would enable the army to crush the PKI without appearing to be the force responsible for ending Guided Democracy.
4. Quoted in Legge J D 1973 *Sukarno: A Political Biography* (Penguin, Harmondsworth), p. 398.

stage a successful generals' coup, but in October 1965 Suharto lacked the personal and political authority to make another coup a realistic possibility. He concentrated at first, therefore, on drawing power to himself gradually. As Commander of KOSTRAD, on the death of Yani he had automatically assumed the position of interim army commander until a permanent replacement had been named. It was thus crucially important for him to refuse to accept Sukarno's appointment of Pranoto as army commander. Because it became clear that the army as a whole backed him in rejecting someone of Pranoto's sympathies, Suharto was able to force Sukarno first into officially entrusting him with restoring security and order in the country on 3 October and then into formally appointing him as army commander in place of Pranoto on 14 October. Command of the army was of vital importance to Suharto in establishing his influence within the military, while the authority to restore security and order gave him at least potentially a presidential mandate to intervene at any level of Indonesian society to restore security and order. Interpreted in its broadest possible sense, this authority amounted to a return to martial law and it enabled the army to turn against its main adversary: the PKI.

THE MASSACRES

The abortive coup had been quickly attributed to the PKI. In the polarised political atmosphere of 1965, the complex events were bound to be seen as favouring one side or the other, and the defeat of the coup immediately appeared as a setback for the party. Neither the party's members, however, nor the vast majority of observers were prepared for the ferocity of the retribution which was now unleashed upon the Left. Within days of Untung's submission the killing of PKI members began in the strongly Muslim province of Aceh. By the end of the year, an extended series of massacres was taking place throughout most of the country, with the killing concentrated where the PKI had once been strongest: in the countryside of Java and Bali and on the plantations of North Sumatra. The killing had subsided considerably by March 1966, but further outbreaks continued until 1969.

There appear to be many reasons for the enormous violence which accompanied the removal of the PKI as a political force.

First, the PKI's activities since 1945 had laid up for itself an enormous store of hatred amongst other sections of Indonesian society. The party had taken sides on a wide range of issues, bringing its formidable organisational skills to bear on one side or other in deep-rooted conflicts, and it had created issues where none had seemed previously to exist. In Aceh, the party's followers were loathed as infidels by the local Muslim community; in North Sumatra they were hated by sections of the indigenous Batak community for promoting the interests of the Javanese settlers who worked on the state plantations; in southern Sumatra, local people resented PKI promotion of land rights and government support for impoverished Javanese transmigrant settlers. In the cities of the archipelago, many Chinese fell victim to the PKI's close association with the People's Republic of China. In Bali, the PKI had attacked the practice of Hinduism, desecrating ceremonies and encouraging people to neglect their traditional religious duties. In the countryside of Central and East Java, as already mentioned, the PKI's promotion of land reform won it bitter enemies, but here it was especially detested by orthodox, traditional Muslims because it was most closely associated with the followers of Kejawen, that version of Islam which had intimately blended Islamic doctrine with Hindu and animist elements to create a distinctive belief system. For the majority of orthodox traditional Muslims, such beliefs were not just blasphemous but close to black magic, and they regarded the PKI and its peasants with a combination of disgust and fear. In parts of East Java, moreover, the party went as far as supporting conversion from Kejawen to Hinduism, adding apostasy to the perceived crimes of the party.

As well as these longstanding hatreds, the PKI faced a sudden sharp increase in antipathy because of what people believed to be the circumstances of the attempted coup. To begin with, Nasution's young daughter was fatally wounded in crossfire during the attempt to arrest her father. The incident was clearly an accident, but it seemed to highlight the carelessness with which the plotters viewed human life. Then, the partially decayed state of the generals' bodies when they were exhumed shortly after the coup quickly gave rise to rumours that the victims had been tortured and mutilated before and after being killed. These rumours soon elaborated into extravagant stories in which the generals' eyes had been poked out and their genitals cut off by wild communist women who then danced naked by firelight before abandoning themselves to the audience of communists and airforce personnel. Fearfulness mounted as new rumours circulated that the communists had dug holes throughout Indonesia in preparation for the bodies of their victims and that they had laid up stocks of implements such as eye-gougers with which to torture their victims before death.

This hysterical fear had little, if any, basis in reality. Whatever involvement Aidit and the Special Bureau may have had in the events in Jakarta, the PKI had made no effort to prepare for a mass uprising and the rank and file party membership were as unprepared for the coup as their anti-communist rivals. The rumours of torture and debauchery at Halim were indeed only rumours – the PKI had always been rather puritanical in sexual matters – while the body-holes and eye-gougers were imaginative elaborations of mundane phenomena: rubbish holes, rubber tapping implements and the like. But the Indonesian people were ready for a culprit. The twenty years since 1945 had been a profound disappointment for virtually everyone: the high hopes of independence had given way to economic collapse and political confrontation. The official rhetoric of Guided Democracy offered little explanation of what had gone wrong, beyond putting the blame on distant NEKOLIM and, indeed, listening to Sukarno's speeches one would hardly suppose that anything was wrong. The Indonesian people were ready to believe that a demonic force was responsible for their plight and the attempted coup enabled them to identify the PKI as their tormentor. Once that label had been firmly fixed to the party in the hours and days after the coup, a violent outbreak against the PKI was inevitable.

The carnage, nonetheless, might not have been so great had the army not chosen to permit and encourage it. The army's initial goal had been to have the PKI banned as punishment for its alleged part in the attempted coup. Sukarno, however, steadfastly refused to agree. Although he became mildly critical of the coup plotters, he realised that to abandon the PKI outright would bring him perilously close to admitting that NASAKOM and other pillars of Guided Democracy had been wrong. To give way to Suharto on this issue would signal his end as the great arbitrator of Indonesian politics. While Sukarno stalled on banning the PKI, Suharto's supporters began to increase pressure by permitting mass actions against the party. This began on 8 October 1965, when the PKI headquarters in Jakarta was attacked and burnt by an anti-communist mob; it quickly descended into mass killing.

Impatient with Sukarno's intractability, the army commanders then turned the killing into their own tool for the PKI's destruction. The PKI's twofold recovery – from repression by the Dutch and Japanese and from defeat in the Madiun affair – already had a somewhat legendary quality, and the army was determined that the destruction this time should be thorough. Recruiting the Indonesian masses was perhaps appealing because of the scale of the destruction to be carried out; the Indonesian army may have lacked the logistical capacity on its own to undertake the elimination of the PKI's cadre thoroughly and quickly, though not long after it was able to shepherd further hundreds of thousands of suspects through interrogations and prison camps. In many regions, the army recruited local vigilantes, drawn from the local anti-communist communities – Muslims in East Java, Christians in North Sulawesi, Hindus in Bali, and so on – gave them weapons, basic training and sometimes a rudimentary uniform, and sent them out to exterminate the communists in their region. Only in West Java, where the army had just finished suppressing the Darul Islam rebellion and had no wish to rearm Muslims, did the army discourage these vigilante killings.[5]

As the killings gathered pace, however, they quickly took on an extra meaning in the consolidation of Suharto's coalition for a new order in Indonesia. One of Suharto's greatest difficulties as he attempted to build his power base was in being sure of the loyalty of his allies. The opacity of politics under Guided Democracy – the very phenomenon which had protected him on the night of the kidnappings – meant that he had great difficulty in identifying reliable supporters outside his immediate circle. Uncertain of his own intelligence organisations, he even seems to have used CIA information in identifying PKI infiltrators within his operation.[6] The killings, however, soon provided an alternative test of loyalty. A willingness to take part in the slaughter was a sign that one was indeed anti-communist and across the archipelago tens of thousands of people whose compromises with Guided Democracy had given them a dubious background now took to the killing fields

---

5. It has been widely reported that the army also restrained the killing in Bali, but there is no reliable evidence that this was the case.
6. See Cribb R 1990 Problems in the Historiography of the Killings in Indonesia. In Cribb R (ed.) *The Indonesian Killings of 1965–1966* (Monash University Centre of Southeast Asian Studies, Clayton), p. 7, note 11.

as a way of demonstrating that they, too, had been enemies of the communists. Participation could even be used to impose loyalty. Anyone who joined in the killings was irrevocably committed to the army's side and on some occasions the close relatives of PKI members were forced to act as executioners so that they would carry a large part of the guilt of murder.

No one can say for certain how many were killed during these terrible months. Reasoned estimates range from 100,000 to a million; a figure of 450,000–500,000 seems plausible and is accepted by the Indonesian government. The victims included the PKI leader Aidit and most of the party's senior leadership, though a couple were saved for public trials and subsequent execution and a few managed to escape abroad. Not all the victims were 'guilty' in the flexible terms of the time – private quarrels were sometimes avenged, family members of party activists were sometimes included in the massacres, and, no doubt, there were cases of mistaken identity. The killing, however, was visited primarily on the Left, and succeeded in eliminating a large part of the cadre of the PKI and its affiliated organisations, so that when the party was finally banned in March 1966 there remained virtually nothing to be dismantled.

THE SLOW FALL OF SUKARNO

The unimpeded physical destruction of the PKI meant that Guided Democracy could never be restored in its original form. It also seriously damaged Sukarno's standing, for it exposed his inability to protect one of his key political supports. Paradoxically, however, it also strengthened his position, for it removed the main focus of unity of the anti-communist alliance, revealing old divisions and disagreements and opening up new possibilities for Sukarno to prevail using his skill at balancing political forces and playing subordinates off against each other. From his position as President-for-Life, Sukarno could still reach out to the mass of the Indonesian people and even to Suharto's immediate subordinates in the army. He retained control of the cabinet and he had lost none of his self-confidence. He appeared to command the personal loyalty of the mass of the Indonesian people while his teachings remained the reference point for all political activity.

On Suharto's side, by contrast, what was coming to be called the New Order coalition, comprising forces which wanted a radical departure from the practices of Guided Democracy, was a loose assemblage of antagonistic political forces: fundamentalist and orthodox Muslims from the legal Nahdatul Ulama and the illegal Masjumi, modernising nationalists from the banned PSI, conservative bureaucrats, anti-communist leftists from the banned Murba, anti-communist student and youth groups led by the University students' organisation KAMI, and ambitious and idealistic military figures. It was a coalition reminiscent in many respects of the Indonesian nationalist movement in the 1930s and 1940s, encompassing fundamentally contradictory views but united by a passionate opposition to a single enemy, the communists now taking the place of the Dutch. And just as nationalist unity had begun to fracture as victory came in sight, the unity of the New Order coalition became more fragile as the PKI disappeared from the scene.

Neither Suharto nor any other member of his coalition was in a position to put forward a blueprint for a new Indonesia at this stage. The political initiative therefore remained with Sukarno. The challenge for Sukarno was whether anything resembling Guided Democracy could be put together without the PKI. The dilemma was that if he attempted to retain the PKI as part of the Guided Democracy formula then the New Order coalition would consolidate and perhaps sweep him from power altogether; if on the other hand he jettisoned the communists, he would lose his main political counterweight against the army.

By November 1965 the outlines of Sukarno's strategy were becoming clear. First, he began to place some distance between himself and the PKI. He still resisted banning the party and he tried to stem the tide of killing in the countryside, saying 'If we go on as we are, brothers, we are going to hell, really we are going to hell.'[7] He also continued to speak highly of the party in public, praising its contribution to the national struggle since Dutch times. But he offered mild criticism of the party's role in the attempted coup and, more importantly, made it clear that the PKI itself was not an essential part of his political vision, telling the public that 'KOM does not mean the PKI, no' and insisting that NASAKOM was a union of ideologies, not parties.[8]

Second, he began to draw together the threads of a new political coalition, based on the Sukarnoist Left and drawing in other

7. Speech, 18 December 1965, quoted in Crouch H 1978 *The Army and Politics in Indonesia* (Cornell University Press, Ithaca), p. 157.
8. Speech, 20 November 1965, quoted ibid., p. 162.

political forces. The other legal political parties were for the most part happy to see the communists removed, for the PKI was a dangerous rival, but they were not uncomfortable with the byzantine political manoeuvrings of Guided Democracy and they saw no especial advantage in a return to martial law. The army's record in its relations with political parties was not one which would immediately encourage the parties to expect a better deal under army rule. Parties such as the PNI and the Nahdatul Ulama, therefore, began at least to talk to Sukarno about their place in the changing order.

Third, he began a determined programme to keep the armed forces off balance by playing upon their internal divisions and summoning up personal loyalties. The senior ranks of the armed forces contained many men who owed a debt of loyalty or gratitude to Sukarno for favours in the past. There was a limit to how comprehensively such debts could be called in, but Sukarno could still exercise great influence when he asked an individual officer for a favour. He appealed, moreover, to those who for one reason or another found the prospect of a victory by Suharto and the New Order coalition unpalatable. Suharto's personal support amongst surviving senior officers of the armed forces was limited by the fear that he might promote his own followers at their expense if he were to become too powerful. The leadership of the airforce, navy and police, in particular, feared the consequences for their forces if an army-dominated government were to come to power. Many officers looked askance, too, at some of Suharto's allies, the fundamentalist Muslims and the modernising nationalists tainted by the Darul Islam and PRRI–Permesta rebellions, and they feared that the displacement of Sukarno might send Indonesian politics spinning out of control in another unpalatable direction.

And finally, Sukarno sought to stem the steady decline in his authority by calling, as it were, for a vote of confidence in his leadership, challenging his military and civilian rivals to oppose him publicly or commit themselves definitively to his leadership. On 15 January 1966 he called on his followers to form *barisan* (ranks or fronts) in his defence, and his principal lieutenants quickly announced the creation of a *Barisan* Sukarno to unite all loyal forces in Indonesia behind their president.

Sukarno's final effort to present the Indonesian public with a new vision of Guided Democracy came on 21 February 1966, when he announced a new cabinet. It was part a bold initiative, part a desperate cobbling together of real and potential allies. He dismissed Nasution as Defence Minister and, in parallel armed forces appointments, moved acknowledged Sukarnoist officers into positions of power. But the cabinet swelled to a hundred members, many of them appointed to conciliate or recruit particular groups. Minister of State for People's Security was Imam Sjafe'i, a powerful boss in the Jakarta underworld, whose task was widely believed to be controlling the city's streets for the Sukarnoists.

In the end, however, Sukarno's strategy failed. He refused to move far enough from the PKI and the Left in general to break up the New Order coalition's determination to reshape Indonesian politics in a fundamental way. Sukarno's defence of the PKI, which had included claims that 'their sacrifices in Indonesia's struggle for freedom were greater than the sacrifices of other parties and other groups',[9] alienated his military sympathisers who held it as an article of faith that the army's contribution to the struggle exceeded all others. At the same time, he was unable to weld a convincing coalition out of the groups hostile to military rule. The chief beneficiaries of Sukarno's attempt to broaden the Guided Democracy coalition were not groups such as the Nahdatul Ulama, who might have been won over from the ranks of the New Order to a system purged of the communists, but rather the Sukarnoist Left, especially the Foreign Minister Subandrio and the Third Deputy Prime Minister Chaerul Saleh, who moved into the forefront as the chief representatives of the government. The Barisan Sukarno, too, was thwarted by the Sukarno's military opponents in a cunning manoeuvre. Rather than opposing the Barisan, the military announced that the entire Indonesian people already supported Sukarno, that the people themselves were effectively already a *barisan* in support of the president and that therefore no physical organisation was necessary to carry out the Barisan's aims.

The main political transformation during the months from October 1965 to March 1966, therefore, aside from the elimination of the PKI, was not so much a formal erosion of Sukarno's authority but rather the growing determination of the Suharto group to remove Sukarno from power as a prelude to a thorough-going political restructuring of the country and their growing confidence that this could be achieved, if handled carefully, without sparking either civil war or a counter-coup. The cabinet announcement of 21 February 1966 was the critical event which

9. Speech, 21 December 1965, quoted in Crouch 1978, p. 164.

prompted the army to act, but Sukarno's fate had been sealed by his inability to break out of the mould of Guided Democracy.

The Suharto forces needed, nonetheless, a pretext for their final seizure of power, and this came from their allies in the student and youth groups. These groups had spearheaded the initial outbreak of violence against the PKI in Jakarta in October 1965, and had mounted a series of street demonstrations in January 1966 to protest against rising prices in particular and the economic incompetence of the government in general. Protected and encouraged by the army, the students took to the streets again in February in an escalating series of rallies first against those ministers, especially Subandrio, seen as typifying the new cabinet's leftist orientation, then against the Department of Foreign Affairs, which Subandrio headed, and finally against buildings connected with the Chinese embassy. Sukarno himself was still immune from direct attack, but his personal authority was clearly no longer sufficient to keep order in the streets of Jakarta. New rumours began to spread, moreover, that student and/or army groups were planning to kidnap and kill Subandrio and the other leftist ministers. With half a million communists already dead and anti-communist indignation raised by the shooting of two demonstrators by Tjakrabirawa troops during a demonstration against the cabinet, this threat seemed real.

Recognising, therefore, that for the moment he had run out of initiatives, and refusing to put his closest colleagues at further risk, Sukarno capitulated. On 11 March 1966, at a meeting in Bogor with three senior generals, Sukarno signed an order instructing Suharto

> to take all measures considered necessary to guarantee security, calm, and stability of the government and the revolution, and to guarantee the personal safety and authority of the President/Supreme Commander/Great Leader of the Revolution/Mandatory of the MPRS [Parliament] in the interests of the unity of the Republic of Indonesia and to carry out all teachings of the Great Leader of the Revolution.[10]

Sukarno may have hoped that he would later be able to manoeuvre his way out of this instruction, but in the end it marked the finish of his effective power. Because the instruction authorised 'all measures' it amounted to a transfer of presidential authority from Sukarno to Suharto. And Suharto's first decree 'in the name of the

10. Quoted ibid., p. 189.

110

president' was to ban the PKI, an act of little practical significance but immense symbolism.

The final dissolution of Guided Democracy was nonetheless a gradual process, as Suharto and his circle moved cautiously to avoid any action which might precipitate a Sukarnoist counter-coup or intra-armed forces civil war. Subandrio and twelve other ministers were arrested a few days after the Bogor incident, and on 30 March 1966 a new cabinet was installed, although none of the new appointees was a dedicated opponent of Sukarno and the president continued to speak freely on public affairs. A purge of the armed forces was begun, but was limited at first to the most prominent left-wing officers, though the Tjakrabirawa palace guard was abolished altogether. Only in June 1966 did Suharto summon the national parliament to set the seal on his political power. At his bidding, the members endorsed the instruction of 11 March (meaning that Sukarno could not revoke it), rescinded Sukarno's appointment as President-for-Life, though without removing him as president, and banned him from issuing presidential decrees.

The final removal of Sukarno was possible, however, only after the slow purge of senior military ranks was well-advanced and only after Sukarno's personal standing had been further eroded by a series of show trials of his main subordinates, especially Subandrio and the former banking minister Jusuf Muda Dalam. The trials, which saw both ministers found guilty and sentenced to death,[11] drove home Sukarno's political powerlessness, but they were more significant for the inside view they purported to give of Guided Democracy and for the hints they dropped that Sukarno himself was involved in the attempted coup. Jusuf's trial in particular revealed gross mismanagement, corruption and disregard for the public's welfare at the most senior levels of government which sullied Sukarno's reputation as a defender of the interests of the little people. Even so the parliamentary session in March 1967 at which Sukarno's hold on the presidency was finally revoked took place in an atmosphere of extreme tension, with rumours circulating widely about possible action in support of the president from Sukarnoist units. Suharto was appointed Acting President and Sukarno was placed under house arrest until his death in June 1970.

11. These sentences were never carried out; Jusuf Muda Dalam died in prison in 1976 and Subandrio's sentence was commuted to life imprisonment.

CHAPTER EIGHT

Politics Suspended, 1966–73

The coalition which came together to oust Sukarno and to destroy the PKI had a good deal in common with the nationalist coalition which had earlier combined to fight the Dutch. Both were alliances between widely differing social forces and ideological standpoints, made possible by the desperate need to unite against a powerful enemy. In 1966, as in 1949, the broad nature of the coalition left unresolved what the alliance might do when it came to power, and this vagueness allowed all concerned to dream enthusiastically of the opportunities the new order might hold for them. The exuberant optimism which had accompanied the Dutch surrender in late 1949 flickered once again amongst the ashes of Guided Democracy.

Key features of the Indonesian political landscape, however, had changed since the end of the war of independence. The political parties were dramatically weakened. The PSI had faded to a shadowy aspiration in the minds of its former supporters after six years of illegality; the Masjumi, also illegal since 1960, had more popular support but its leaders quickly showed themselves unable to cope with the New Order political climate; the PNI had been gutted by the purge of its more left-wing members; the PKI, once the best organised of all, had disappeared in the appalling bloodshed of 1965–66; and all the remaining parties had suffered from loss of access to power and influence under Guided Democracy. There was no leader of the opposition, no government-in-exile ready to step into power once Sukarno was prised out of it. The constitution of 1950 which had handed political power to the party-dominated parliament, moreover, had been set aside under Sukarno in favour of the 1945 presidential constitution. Suharto made no move whatsoever to reverse this position. Not even by default could political power return to the parties.

At the same time, the armed forces were vastly more powerful than they had been in 1949. Almost constant military action in one part or other of the archipelago since 1950, together with a long-term concentration of power into the hands of the high command had turned the armed forces, especially the army, into a coherent and disciplined force. Most army divisions continued to recruit primarily within their own regions, and local loyalties remained strong, but a unified officer-training programme, together with Nasution's rotation of commanding officers, had begun to produce homogeneity. The officer corps, moreover, although dominated by Javanese, was drawn from a range of ethnic groups wide enough to back the army's claim to be a truly national institution. Alongside the regular divisional structure, moreover, the high command had sponsored a number of well-supplied and thoroughly trained elite formations, including the Strategic Reserve (KOSTRAD), the paracommandos (RPKAD) and the marines (KKO), whose independence of regional ties made them more reliable. Military supply had suffered during the economic disintegration of late Guided Democracy, and spare parts for much of the equipment acquired from the Soviet Union became difficult to obtain, but the armed forces' domination of the state budget since the late 1950s and the extra income from the nationalised industries they controlled meant that they were vastly better equipped than any of their civilian counterparts. And of course, the military had already tasted extensive political power during the period of martial law which marked the start of Guided Democracy.

The initiative for the shaping of post-Sukarno Indonesia, therefore, lay with Suharto and a small circle of generals whom he trusted. Suharto and his group, however, had no interest in allowing the elimination of the PKI to clear the way for another of the country's rival ideologies to attempt to impose its vision of the soul of Indonesia. The new military rulers hated and despised the communist party, and thus communism, but they had no affection for the other ideologies which had contended in the 1950s. Islam was compromised in their eyes by its association with the Darul Islam insurgency; modernising nationalism, although in many ways the army's natural ally, was tainted by its connections with the PRRI–Permesta uprising; conservative revivalist nationalism seemed to offer no prospect of leading the country out of poverty

113

and traditionalism towards prosperity and modernity. And all of these ideologies and their attached parties shared responsibility, in the military's view, for the country's predicament. Suharto saw the parties of the 1950s and their parliamentary representatives as having pursued purely selfish political agendas, defending their own interests and thwarting the broader needs of society. He saw the liberal system of the 1950s as responsible for the rise of the communist party and the chaos of the early 1960s, and was determined that what was increasingly called New Order Indonesia would not be permitted to return to those times of dissension and division. In planning the New Order, therefore, he took as his starting point that correct policies would only be followed by a government which was sufficiently insulated from sectional interests and public opinions to enable it to pursue policy in the national interest.

Suharto was able to spurn the parties because his position rested primarily on military power. No force outside the armed forces could possibly topple him, and his careful accumulation of power between 1965 and 1967 ensured that for the moment he faced no serious challenge from within the military. His scorn for ideology and his rejection of politics, however, was also politically astute. He sensed a weariness with politics in large sections of the population. The strident insistence on political conformity under Guided Democracy and the horrifying consequences of political engagement during the coup and the massacres had left many Indonesians longing for an end to ideology as the driving force in politics and government. Suharto was able to turn his lack of political credentials and experience, and his dour, unexciting personality into a powerful political tool appealing to a population jaded with Sukarnoist politics. When he sought civilian political allies, he turned to figures who had stood a little to the side of conventional politics. The Sultan of Yogyakarta, Hamengku Buwono IX, who became the New Order's first coordinator of economic affairs, had extensive experience in government and administration but was not directly linked with any party; Adam Malik, Suharto's first Foreign Minister, had been something of a political maverick since the war of independence, a skilled politician but not a man of the party machines. These two men, together with Suharto, were sometimes described as a triumvirate, but it was no alliance of equals. Only Suharto had a significant power base, and it was on Suharto's terms that they joined the government.

To set the seal on this deliberate disavowal of politics, Suharto turned, as Sukarno had turned before him, to the Pancasila. It became common to refer to the New Order as 'Pancasila Democracy', but this term, like the Pancasila itself, was virtually devoid of practical meaning. As in 1945, the Pancasila offered no programme or guide to action. Rather, it was simply a promise that no single ideology would prevail, that the stalemate which advantaged none and disadvantaged none would be retained, so that ideological differences could be set to one side while other tasks were carried out.

ECONOMIC DEVELOPMENT

In 1945 the task at hand had been defending independence against the Dutch. In 1966 the task defined by the Suharto government was development, or *pembangunan*. To Indonesia's new military rulers, development meant aspiring to the twin aims of prosperity and modernity by employing technology and sound management. The policies meant to achieve this were negotiated between the army and a group of Indonesian economic managers or technocrats, headed by Professor Widjojo Nitisastro.[1] The technocrats worked from within the powerful National Development Planning Board, BAPPENAS,[2] which kept in close touch with the latest in economic thinking in the United States and Europe. The central feature of the development policy which was finally adopted was a series of five-year plans intended to put an orderly and lasting structure into what was forecast to be 'twenty-five years of accelerated modernisation'. The obstacles to this ambitious programme were formidable. Inflation had reached 640 per cent during 1966; in April 1966, the country owed US $2,358 million to foreign creditors, and had virtually no foreign exchange reserves. Its anticipated export earnings of $430 million in 1966 would not have been enough even to service the debt. The country's infrastructure was badly decayed, while investment in plantations

1. An American radical scholar, David Ransome, named them collectively the 'Berkeley Mafia' to draw attention to their connections with the United States, and specifically with the University of California, Berkeley. See David Ransome, 'The Berkeley Mafia and the Indonesian massacres', *Ramparts*, 9 (4), 1970, pp. 27–9, 40–9. In fact, only a few of these men had studied at Berkeley, but most were certainly heirs to the American tradition of thinking on economic development.
2. Badan Perencanaan Pembangunan Nasional.

and industries had been neglected since independence. Per capita income was $50 p.a., and Indonesia had become one of the poorest countries in the world.

The initial aim of the technocrats was to save the country from bankruptcy by rescheduling the foreign debt and obtaining new loan funds to sustain the government while longer-term policies were put into place. A long series of negotiations began with creditors, resulting in a gradual reopening of credit to Indonesia and finally in the establishment of an international consortium, the Inter-Governmental Group on Indonesia (IGGI), to coordinate aid and credit to Jakarta. This dramatic transformation of Indonesia's creditworthiness was able to take place because the technocrats adopted stringent economic policies which Western financiers regarded as sound. In particular, the technocrats tackled inflation, bringing the rate down to single figures by 1969. The new rulers also overturned Sukarno's nationalist hostility to foreign economic involvement in the Indonesian economy, returning some nationalised foreign enterprises and passing a Foreign Investment Law in 1967 which was designed to attract foreign capital with generous provisions on the questions of local control and sending of profits abroad.

The drive for foreign capital focused especially on natural resources. More than forty agreements with foreign oil companies were signed in order to get production re-established quickly, while large areas of tropical rainforest were handed over in logging concessions. From the early 1970s, foreign investment in manufacturing began to reach significant levels, making the most of the still-generous investment regulations as well as the now-compliant workforce.

These measures were ideologically painful. Indonesian nationalists were deeply uncomfortable with the close economic scrutiny which lenders now insisted upon, and they were thoroughly uneasy about permitting foreign enterprise to regain any of the economic power which it had lost during the nationalisations of the 1950s and 1960s. The search for international respectability also led to the end of the Confrontation with Malaysia in August 1966. Indonesia's military leaders had always had misgivings about a campaign they did not expect to win, but the abandonment of Confrontation was hastened by the need to placate the controllers of international finance. Indonesia's return to international respectability was finally sealed in September 1966 when it rejoined the United Nations.

Indonesia under Suharto did not entirely abandon its ambitions for international influence, but it limited them severely, muting its participation in the Non-Aligned Movement and other world bodies and instead concentrating on its own region. In 1967, Indonesia joined Malaysia, the Philippines, Singapore and Thailand to form ASEAN, the Association of Southeast Asian Nations. ASEAN's members were all anti-communist and the organisation's initial intention was to strengthen the internal resilience of the member states by cooperating in regional economic development. Relatively little has come of this economic cooperation, but ASEAN has developed instead into an influential diplomatic caucus, in which each country has been able to recruit the support of its fellow members over issues on which it feels strongly. From a position of some strength as host to the permanent ASEAN Secretariat, Indonesia has been able to press for policies to reduce the presence of outside forces in the Southeast Asian region. Working partly through ASEAN, for instance, Indonesia played an important role in the diplomatic process which led to democratic elections in Cambodia in 1993 and to a reduction in direct Chinese backing for the former Khmer Rouge rulers of the country.

The capital generated by new credit and foreign aid, by foreign investment and by the sale of natural resources enabled Indonesia to invest once more in infrastructure. Roads, telecommunications, ports, hotels, electric power facilities and the like were put into place to service the new economy, and basic industries such as cement, fertiliser and textile production were supported.

In the countryside, the government relaunched an ambitious programme to achieve self-sufficiency in rice production: the so-called 'Green Revolution'. Drawing on the most recent biological research, the programme introduced new high-yielding varieties of rice to Indonesian farmers, together with modern chemical fertilisers and pesticides, machinery, expanded irrigation facilities and extensive technical advice. By 1969 the programme covered more than two million hectares of rice-producing land. Where all these factors were delivered more or less as planned, the result was a dramatic increase in productivity. Individual crops were larger, and farmers who had grown one crop a year were able to produce up to five crops in two years: average production per hectare rose from 2.6 tonnes in 1968 to 4.8 in 1985.

In many areas, however, the programme faced significant problems. The new varieties of rice were often more vulnerable

117

than the old to disease and unseasonable weather; many also were less tasty than traditional varieties and commanded lower prices at market. The system was dependent on reliable supplies of seed, pesticide and fertiliser, but corruption and inefficiency in the supply networks was a major problem. Although the programme was actively promoted by the government, moreover, farmers were expected to pay for many of the inputs. They were promised credit from government banks to enable them to make the necessary purchases, but for many farmers living close to the subsistence level, either the interest rates were too high or the risks too great to permit them to participate in the programme. Serious environmental problems emerged, too: overuse of pesticides and fertilisers, which were often distributed without adequate instruction, led to the poisoning of people, farm animals, and fishponds, as well as the wildlife which once fed upon the pests of the rice crop. The now-continuous growing season for rice, moreover, meant that the life cycle of various insect pests was no longer broken by the annual harvest and fallowing of fields; from 1969 Java, in particular, was swept by plagues of insects which not only ate the leaves of the rice plants but transmitted major viral diseases of rice. These environmental problems were solved only in the late 1980s with the introduction of a programme of integrated pest management involving the abandonment of many pesticides and the reintroduction of older pest-resistant rice varieties and other techniques of biological control.

The New Order government also took up enthusiastically the policy of transmigration, the shifting of people from the densely populated islands of Java and Bali to the ostensibly underpopulated outer islands of the archipelago. This policy had been attempted on a small scale by the Dutch colonial authorities and Sukarno had taken it up in the 1960s, announcing an annual target of 1.5 million people to be shifted. The New Order and its foreign sponsors found the idea of redistributing population as captivating as their predecessors had done, and devoted time, energy and foreign aid to surveying and preparing sites in Sumatra, Kalimantan and elsewhere, and to shifting whole families with their possessions to a new life in the wilderness, though it took the New Order from 1969 to 1982 to shift the 1.5 million people Sukarno had planned to move in a single year.

When properly managed, the transmigration programme achieved many of its aims, but as with the Green Revolution there was much scope for miscalculation and neglect. Sites were selected in the jungle with little regard for the traditional hunting or shifting cultivation rights of local people. Some sites were utterly unsuitable because of susceptibility to flooding or other problems, while in many areas the soil exposed after lush tropical rainforest had been cleared became infertile after a few seasons' cultivation. Some transmigrants arrived at their designated sites to find little or no preparatory work had been done to receive them, and others found that the support they had been promised during the first months until they were established did not materialise. Most discouraging of all, it rapidly became clear that transmigration was having only a limited impact on the population of Java. During the thirteen years it took to move 1.5 million people from Java the island's population grew by seventeen million.

The inadequacy of transmigration focused attention on the broad issue of family planning. Sukarno, although keen to re-distribute the Indonesian population, had wanted greater numbers to strengthen Indonesia's credentials as a great power. Suharto, however, soon launched a programme to reduce the rate of population growth by spreading awareness of modern contra-ceptive techniques amongst the mass of the people. The National Family Planning Cooperation Board, established in 1970, con-centrated on public information and persuasion, providing advice and free contraceptive services through a network of centres and clinics especially in the countryside. Although isolated instances of coercion have been reported, Indonesia's reliance on persuasion presents a striking contrast with the coercive measures used to support family planning in India and China. The family planning campaign was also dramatically successful, reducing for instance the average number of children born to Balinese women from 5.8 to 3.8.

Each of these campaigns – the Green Revolution, transmigra-tion and family planning – worked within the New Order as a kind of substitute for politics. They were initiated by the government to solve readily identifiable problems, and they therefore enabled the government to point to its concern for social welfare even when its other policies were causing difficulty and deprivation. Each of the campaigns, moreover, put before idealistic Indonesians a problem, a goal and a programme for achieving the goal which provided a channel for action. They gave a generation of Indonesians a sense of participation in their country's future which the political system refused them.

The presence of these campaigns alongside the New Order's

longer-term policies encouraged Suharto to expect that the policies of development and stability would provide their own justification. He looked forward to an Indonesia which would be socially just and prosperous, and he believed that achieving development would vindicate an authoritarian style of government. He realised from the start, however, that his policies would not satisfy all Indonesians and that he needed a political format to support his initiatives. Although the New Order government continued to make much of its economic performance, the regime soon came to rest at least as much on the twin pillars of political repression and controlling political participation.

THE POLITICAL FORMAT

Political repression, of course, had begun with the violent suppression of the PKI, but although the Indonesian armed forces were to be involved in a number of massacres of political opponents on a smaller scale in later years, the model for New Order repression was not the mass killings of 1965–66 but the even more extensive imprisonment of leftists after the killings. Over one and a half million Indonesians – the New Order government's own figure – passed through detention camps in the aftermath of the 1965 coup. Some were tried and convicted, receiving sentences ranging from death to varying terms of imprisonment. Many were detained only briefly. But hundreds of thousands spent months or years in prison camps dotted about the archipelago. The best known complex of camps was on the isolated island of Buru in eastern Indonesia, where detainees were set to work carving new settlements out of the jungle. Because of the numbers involved and the difficulty in obtaining evidence, the vast majority of detainees were not tried but were held administratively on the grounds that they had been 'involved' in the 1965 coup. 'Involvement' was interpreted very broadly to encompass any kind of connection with the PKI and its ideas during the years of Guided Democracy. This criterion, however, was so vague, and the PKI's engagement in politics in the early 1960s so comprehensive, that it soon became a convenient general tool which could be used selectively to remove from politics anyone on the Left. The new rulers, too, later discovered the value of anti-subversion regulations inherited from the Dutch and from the Sukarno era, which defined offences against the political order in terms so vague that they simply gave the authorities carte blanche to discipline anyone they judged to be dangerous to their interests.

The principal tools for this repression were two institutions, BAKIN and KOPKAMTIB.[3] BAKIN was a nominally civilian intelligence organisation, though in practice it was heavily dominated by seconded military officers, with the task of maintaining surveillance of the civilian community in order to track down dangerous dissent for referral to the security forces. KOPKAMTIB, by contrast, was a special security command set up within the armed forces on the basis of Sukarno's October 1965 instruction to Suharto to restore security and order. Its structure had enabled Suharto to establish his own formal lines of communication within the armed forces without setting aside the existing hierarchy, while its broad mandate gave the military general legal authority for any action it judged to be in the interests of the state. KOPKAMTIB became an instrument for internal security, rather than part of Suharto's direct power base in 1969, when he handed command over to General Maraden Panggabean, but it remained a rubric for the internal security operations of the armed forces as a whole, rather than a distinct security apparatus. In practice the functions of BAKIN and KOPKAMTIB tended to overlap, while the police and other sections of the armed forces were also engaged in security work alongside their main tasks.

Repression alone, however, was not enough. The widespread disillusionment with politics and ideology which assisted Suharto in his first months in power began to evaporate, and discussion on the appropriate long-term system for New Order Indonesia became more insistent. The political formats offered for debate varied widely in the number of parties they proposed to tolerate and the form of elections they proposed to hold, but they all assumed some form of mass democratic participation in politics. The New Order's international sponsors, too, left no doubt that they expected some form of democratic restoration in Indonesia, though they did not specify a timetable or a structure.

The military establishment also began to look on limited democratisation as a way of defusing discontent with some of its policies. A number of the key decisions taken by the technocrats early in the New Order, such as allowing prices to rise, had caused major hardship and consequent resentment amongst the urban

3. BAKIN, Badan Koordinasi Intelijen Negara, State Board for Intelligence Coordination; KOPKAMTIB, Komando Operasi Pemulihan Keamanan dan Ketertiban, Operational Command for the Restoration of Security and Order.

poor and lower middle classes. The lack of restriction on executive power, too, began to affect the mass of the people. Development projects inevitably required government decisions on siting and other aspects of new infrastructure, and officials, now freed from the political need to take account of public opinion, were often ruthless in their planning decisions. The same determined focus on long-term developmental goals and disregard of short-term consequences drove the government's labour policies. In an atmosphere where any challenge to official authority could be labelled communist, few avenues for legal redress were open to the poor. While repression could always pursue the politically engaged, allowing some political participation seemed a prudent strategy to prevent resentment from developing into opposition.

Under these circumstances, the military government became increasingly aware of the need to create a political format which would give the mass of the people some sense of participating in the political process and which would allow serious grievances to receive a hearing before they developed into a security risk, but which would keep the prerogatives of decision-making firmly in the hands of the government. The military government was also constrained by its public commitment to the 1945 Constitution; having dismembered the PKI for allegedly attempting to over-throw the constitution, the military could hardly dismantle the constitution once it was firmly in power. Although Suharto was in no hurry to set a new political order in place and was happy to implement his development policies using the old Sukarnoist political structures, he found himself pushed steadily towards political reconstruction.

Although the debate on political restructuring began in New Order circles as soon as the communist threat was firmly vanquished, the first clear test of the military's political management skills came in the province of West Irian. The province had been regained under United Nations auspices in 1963 with the proviso that an 'Act of Free Choice' should be held in 1968 to determine whether the inhabitants of the province wished to remain a part of Indonesia. By 1968, however, it was clear that the people of the province were by no means universally enthusiastic about Indonesian rule. Domination of the new administration by outsiders from Java and elsewhere, along with the unconcealed contempt of many Indonesians for traditional indigenous culture, prompted a revolt led by the Free Papua Movement or OPM.[4] Discontent was further fuelled by Indonesia's eagerness to begin exploiting the natural resources of the province. One of the first major foreign investments sponsored by the New Order government had been a huge copper mine in the central mountains of Irian in 1967 under terms which brought little direct benefit to the people of the province.

Suharto put the task of organising and winning the Irian vote in the hands of one of his closest lieutenants, General Ali Murtopo, who headed an organisation called Special Operations or OPSUS.[5] Murtopo undertook a multi-pronged strategy, importing food and other consumer goods in the months before the vote in order to strengthen the impression that Indonesian rule had brought prosperity, and warning surreptitiously at the same time that a decision by the people of the territory against Indonesia would not end Indonesian rule. He also arranged that the Act of Free Choice would not be a plebiscite involving the entire population but would take the form of a consultation with 1,025 selected tribal leaders meeting under Indonesian auspices in July–August 1969. The assembled leaders decided without a formal vote to confirm integration with Indonesia.[6] The Irian example did not directly influence political developments at the national level, but in showing the power of political management it set the tone for the government's reorganisation of the political order.

As we have seen in Chapter 4, the 1945 Constitution provides for a parliament of two chambers. The smaller of these, the DPR, is largely elected and has the general legislative responsibilities of parliament. The larger chamber, the MPR, comprises all members of the DPR together with a roughly equal number of members nominated by the president and other official bodies. The MPR meets once in five years to elect the president and to draft a document called the Broad Outlines of State Policy,[7] which determines the thrust of government policy for the coming five years, but because it is dominated by presidential nominees it presents no problem of control. The central problem for the

---

4. Organisasi Papua Merdeka.
5. Operasi Khusus.
6. The United Nations, which had had no intention that the Act of Free Choice should allow Irian to secede from Indonesia, had never specified the form which the Act should take, and so Indonesia's arrangements involved no breach of international undertakings.
7. Garis Besar Haluan Negara, GBHN.

military government rather was to ensure that it controlled the DPR. Although it could rely upon a bloc of military representatives,[8] the government needed to take direct part in elections to ensure parliamentary control.

Suharto and his colleagues chose as their vehicle for this parliamentary and electoral venture a federation of army-sponsored associations and trade unions called Golkar.[9] Golkar had played a small role under Guided Democracy as an umbrella for civilian anti-communist associations, but it was quickly transformed into an electoral vehicle for the new government. Golkar did not become a party: it had no individual membership, no distinct cadre of activists and no ideology of its own. It was a name against which voters could register support for the government at election time.

National elections, however, had not been held since 1955, and Golkar was an unknown electoral quantity, so the government sought to ensure its own victory with the same degree of careful preparation it had used in Irian. First, independent candidates were banned, along with the micro-parties. This left nine parties in the contest alongside Golkar. Ali Murtopo then took a close hand in the internal affairs of the legal parties, intervening especially to have pro-military figures elected to party leaderships. Perhaps the clearest indication that the government intended to hobble the parties came when former members of the banned Masjumi attempted to reconstitute the modernist Muslim political stream in a new party, the Partai Muslimin Indonesia, or Parmusi. Although he permitted the new party to form, Suharto prohibited former Masjumi leaders from holding office in it, and eventually intervened to appoint one of his own cabinet ministers, Mintaredja, as party head.

Even more important, the government began to purge the bureaucracy systematically of members of the legal parties. Government spokesmen introduced the term 'monoloyalty', arguing that party membership was incompatible with impartial service to the nation and that civil servants who received their livelihood from the government should repay that support by showing loyalty to

8. Members of Indonesia's armed forces are not permitted to vote in elections in order to avoid any direct politicisation of the rank and file. In compensation, the military as a whole is allocated a bloc of seats in the DPR which are filled by nomination. In 1971 these representatives numbered seventy-five out of a DPR of 460.

9. More fully Sekber Golkar, or Sekretariat Bersama Golongan Karya, Joint Secretariat of Functional Groups.

the government at election time. Party members were given six months to resign their membership or leave their jobs. Golkar, however, was not considered to be a party and, as mentioned above, it had no individual membership, and so it was unaffected by these requirements. Moreover, all civil servants were required to belong to a single organisation, Korpri,[10] which was in turn a member of Golkar.

In the election campaign in 1971, Golkar made great use of government officials in the countryside who used their status to win the backing of peasants. Thus when the ballots were counted, Golkar had swept the board with nearly 63 per cent of the vote, winning 227 of the 351 seats at stake. This massive victory undeniably reflected significant public confidence in the new regime, but it also reflected both the effectiveness of the government's efforts to blunt the will of the parties and a carefully cultivated fear of the consequences if the government's drive for electoral success were thwarted. The only party to retain a significant share of its former vote was the Nahdatul Ulama, whose power base lay amongst conservative Muslim communities, especially in densely populated East Java.

The extent of this victory encouraged the government to proceed with a fuller reorganisation of the parties, forcing them to merge into two groupings, which subsequently became two parties in January 1973. The new Indonesian Democratic Party (PDI, Partai Demokrasi Indonesia) encompassed the old PNI, the two Christian parties, the leftist but anti-communist Murba, and the former army-sponsored IPKI. The Unity Development Party (PPP, Partai Persatuan Pembangunan) incorporated the four legal Muslim parties, Nahdatul Ulama, Parmusi and the smaller PERTI and Partai Sarekat Islam Indonesia. Ideologically, the enforced mergers reflected the government's view that parties should not be allowed to reflect narrow sectional interests but should aggregate a broad national consensus. Politically, the mergers worked to cripple the old parties, by pitting their component parts against each other within the new party structures and absorbing their energies in mutually destructive quarrels.

By 1974 the policies of Suharto's New Order had begun to bear fruit in the form of economic growth and dramatically improved infrastructure. Three less palatable features of the New Order,

---

10. Korps Pegawai Republik Indonesia: Civil Servants Corps of the Republic of Indonesia.

however, had also emerged. First, it was clear that there was very little democracy in the government's decision-making process. The parliament was demonstrably in the government's pocket. Government policy emerged from the presidential palace, from BAPPENAS and from the armed forces without an intervening stage of public consultation, and political repression was used to keep dissenting voices quiet. Ali Murtopo and OPSUS, in particular, seemed to symbolise the regime's cynical willingness to resort to manipulation and dirty tricks to achieve its political aims, regardless of public opinion. Whatever benefits the New Order might claim to have delivered, it could not claim that it had given Indonesians a greater sense of controlling their own destinies.

Second, those economic benefits which were the New Order's pride were unevenly distributed. Upper levels of society had prospered enormously as a result of Suharto's policies, and much of the rest of society had benefited from better roads, improved education, more stable food supply, and so on. Most observers agree that the number of Indonesians living in absolute poverty gradually declined. But the gap between rich and poor seemed to have widened and to show no signs of ever narrowing. Development, moreover, had left millions of victims: urban workers sweating in primitive factories with no opportunity to campaign for better conditions; poor farmers forced off their land by crippling debt; householders evicted from their lands with little compensation to make way for development projects.

Third, gross corruption was now found in the upper levels of the elite. The resources boom, combined with the dependence of investors on government permits, had enabled officials in positions colloquially known as 'wet' (*basah*) to enrich themselves enormously. Officials on modest salaries were suddenly able to afford holidays in New York and sumptuous houses in Europe. Wedding ceremonies, which traditionally provide an index of the prosperity of the families involved, became massive, extravagant affairs. Many senior government figures, moreover, including Suharto himself, had developed close ties with so-called *cukong*, Chinese businessmen to whom they fed government favours in exchange for a share of the profits. And the president's wife, Tien, was reputed to be so deeply involved in graft that Jakarta wits described her as 'Madame Tien Percent'.

Impatience was welling up, too, amongst those who had expected different policies of the New Order. The Muslims who had joined the New Order coalition in 1965–66 had not counted on making great gains for Islam under the military-dominated regime, but they were deeply angered by what they saw as the secularising tendencies of the New Order. These ranged from the gradual removal of old-style religious leaders from the ranks of the Ministry of Religion to the apparent susceptibility of Indonesia's youth to Western fashion and custom. Most contentious of all, however, was a new Marriage Law introduced in 1973, which would have set all Indonesian marriages on a purely secular basis and denied the legal applicability of any significant aspect of Islamic marriage law. So hostile was the Muslim reaction to the Marriage Law that it was eventually withdrawn and reintroduced with major amendments to conciliate the Muslims, but the episode did significant damage to the government's overall standing.

Related to this fear of secularisation and Westernisation was a growing unease with the extent of foreign ownership and control in the Indonesian economy. A generation of Indonesians had grown up hearing Sukarno's denunciations of Western capitalism and imperialism, and the New Order government appeared to such people to be selling the country's birthright for short-term gain and to be relegating Indonesia once more to a role as sweated workshop for the industrialised world.

Disquiet over all these shortcomings erupted in January 1974 into demonstrations in Jakarta nominally against the visiting Japanese prime minister, Kakuei Tanaka, but patently directed at the Suharto government. The demonstration broke into violent riots, with Japanese cars and a great many buildings being burnt and an official death toll of eleven people shot by the security forces.

The riots were given the quasi-official name 'Disaster of 15 January' (shortened to Malari from its Indonesian acronym),[11] and indeed it was a disaster from the government's point of view, because it demonstrated that eight years of the New Order had not done away with the basis for violent dissent against official policies. It also showed that Suharto was not immune from criticism from within the ranks of the armed forces: there was strong evidence to suggest that a number of army officers dissatisfied with the directions in which the New Order was moving and led by KOPKAMTIB commander General Sumitro were to some extent involved in the demonstrations. It was the kind of crisis which,

11. Malapetaka Limabelas Januari.

in other countries, has often persuaded military rulers to begin withdrawing from the thankless task of government, and indeed many observers predicted that the New Order regime would lose heart. Suharto, however, responded with a major new initiative to consolidate his rule by establishing a corporate state.

CHAPTER NINE

Towards a Corporate State, 1974–87

The Malari riots did not immediately transform Indonesian politics, but they marked a gradual change of direction. Until Malari, as described in the previous chapter, the New Order regime relied politically on a platform of economic performance, political repression and managed political participation. All three elements of this platform remained in place after 1974, but to them was added a fourth platform of ideological control. The New Order government which had launched itself in 1966 as an administration of non-political managers now began seeking to shape Indonesian society to match its own ideological vision. This change coincided with the growing power of Suharto as president.

The new ideological element was not immediately apparent because the New Order regime responded to Malari first of all by reinforcing its three original pillars. Most striking was a sudden tightening of political repression. In the aftermath of Malari, six of Jakarta's more independent and critical newspapers were summarily banned, three alleged ringleaders of the riots were tried and sentenced under the loosely-worded subversion laws, and a heavy-handed academic, Daoed Joesoef, was appointed minister of education, with the task of depoliticising the universities, whose students had played an important role in the riots.

Indeed, the New Order continued to adopt what many observers saw as a distressing willingness to use heavy-handed methods to enforce its will. Most striking of these were the so-called 'mysterious shootings' (*penembakan misterius*, or *Petrus*) which began in late 1982. Earlier that year, a widespread outbreak of violent crime, especially in the cities, had raised serious questions about the government's capacity to provide a peaceful social environment for development. The killings began as an unexplained series of murders of known and alleged criminals in cities on Java. As the wave of killings spread, it became apparent that they were being carried out with military efficiency by men who looked very much like paracommandos in civilian clothing. The victims, who were apparently identified by the killers from lists, included known criminals, former prisoners and local toughs, as well as some innocent bystanders who were mistakenly identified. Bodies of victims were sometimes disposed of quietly, sometimes left on public display. The government, however, claimed to know nothing of the murders, suggesting ingenuously that they were a result of gang warfare and taking no steps to stop them. During 1983 the killings spread beyond Java to other islands and were extended to the deliberate shooting of escaping or escaped prisoners. A conservative count suggests that several thousand people died in the operation, none of them with anything resembling a trial. Suharto himself finally accepted responsibility for ordering the killings in 1989. So serious had the level of violent crime become before the killings began, however, that many Indonesians actually welcomed the killings as proof that the authorities had decided to 'get tough' on law-breakers. Those who did protest at these drastic measures often found themselves subject to intimidation – an investigative journalist who paid undue attention to the killings had a dead body dumped in his garden as a warning – and the events were a grim reminder of the willingness of the authorities to resort to violence against their enemies.

At the same time, however, the regime responded positively to criticism that its economic policies were too accommodating to foreign capital. It began to close the domestic consumer sector, including formerly lucrative areas such as textile production, to foreign investors, and began directing foreign investment into areas where Indonesians lacked the skill and/or the capital to make significant progress. In May 1975 the government banned new foreign investment in logging and used tax and other incentives to begin channelling timber investors into value-added activities such as pulp, paper and plywood manufacture. The previously generous regulations, which gave foreign investors a high degree of control of their operations, gave way to a requirement that all future foreign investment take the form and substance of joint ventures with Indonesian entrepreneurs.

The political order was also revised with the passing of a new law in 1975 on political parties and Golkar. This formalised regulations, making it virtually impossible for the parties to win an election. First, the law restricted party activity in rural areas, where the bulk of the population still lived, by preventing the parties from establishing branches outside district (*kabupaten*) capitals and by declaring the rural population to be a 'floating mass'. By this term, the government meant that rural people should not be drawn into political activities except at election time, so that they would not be distracted from the tasks of national development, and so that they would be fully responsive to government instruction and advice.

Second, elections became even more tightly controlled. Contestants were not permitted to question the Broad Outlines of State Policy, on the grounds that this had been decided by the MPR as sovereign representative of the Indonesian people, but could only offer comments on how the Broad Outlines had been implemented. To ensure conformity, the parties, along with Golkar, were required to submit all electoral material, especially campaign slogans, in advance for vetting by the electoral commission. The colonial-era laws which prohibited any statement likely to produce discord between racial, social or religious groups, and of course the regulations which banned insulting the head of state were enforced with especial rigour at election time. The commission was also required to vet lists of candidates submitted by the parties and Golkar, and regularly struck off individuals it regarded as undesirable, including sitting members of parliament and of the provincial assemblies who had shown too much independence during their term in office. OPSUS and its successors routinely hampered the activities of the parties, too, making access to facilities difficult and disrupting meetings.

The government also aimed to create a sense of crisis at election time which worked in its own favour. During the six-week official campaign period (reduced to twenty-five days in 1986), some of the restrictions which hamper parties for the rest of the five-year parliamentary term are lifted temporarily, creating an unusual and somewhat unnerving sense of political freedom. Election rallies are permitted, election posters are plastered over buildings and alongside roads. An atmosphere of political competition is conjured up and public figures discuss the likely outcome of the election in terms of percentage votes for Golkar and its rivals. The elections, in short, offer a brief reminder of the politics of the 1950s, but this reminder comes with a scarcely-veiled warning from the government that elections are a time of national peril, a time when the steady course of administration and development is briefly at risk from public misunderstanding of the need for stable government. Most election campaigns have been marred by outbreaks of political violence, especially during mass rallies, although the extent of this violence appeared to be declining by 1987. Elections are presented as a kind of massive national ritual, a 'festival of democracy', but one whose purpose is not so much to choose as to reaffirm faith in the government. For all this manipulation, though, Golkar probably enjoys fairly widespread support, albeit more often passive than active.

EAST TIMOR

Perhaps the most spectacular example of this combination of ruthless repression and political manipulation was Indonesia's forcible annexation of East Timor. In 1974 Portuguese Timor was a neglected overseas territory of Western Europe's poorest country, a relic of Portugal's sixteenth century incursions into the archipelago which had been tolerated in succeeding centuries mainly because Timor was too poor to be worth fighting for. Although some Indonesian nationalists had talked of including East Timor in the new republic in 1945, Indonesia had soon repudiated any claim to the territory. The claim to Western New Guinea was far more important during the 1950s and early 1960s, and Indonesia could not afford to undermine the public position that it was the legal heir to all of, and nothing more than, the former Netherlands Indies. In 1974, however, after an armed forces coup in Lisbon overthrew the Caetano regime, a new Portuguese government announced that all overseas territories would receive the right of self-determination. Political activity stirred in East Timor, coalescing around the UDT,[1] which proposed greater autonomy within a continuing relationship with Portugal and no more than gradual change to the social status quo, and the ASDT, later Fretilin,[2] which advocated immediate independence and thoroughgoing social reform. Other minor parties emerged to call for integration with Australia or Indonesia, or for the restoration of power to traditional chiefs (*liurai*), but politics rapidly polarised around rivalry between UDT and Fretilin.

1. União Democrática Timorense: Timorese Democratic Union.
2. Frente Revolucionária do Timor Leste Independente: Revolutionary Front for an Independent East Timor.

At this point, Indonesia became alarmed, fearing that the left-wing Fretilin might succeed in establishing a communist regime on Indonesia's borders. This alarm grew as it became clear that Portugal, distracted by its own internal political turmoil, had no intention of guiding political events, and was intensified by the fall of Cambodia, South Vietnam and Laos to communist forces during 1975. Alongside these fears were worries that a viable independent East Timor might encourage regional secessionist movements within Indonesia. Meanwhile, the success of OPSUS in managing such affairs as the 'Act of Free Choice' in Western New Guinea and the 1971 national elections encouraged the New Order to believe in the effectiveness of covert political management, and in order to keep a hand in Timorese affairs, Indonesia began to fund and support the minor Apodeti party, which advocated integration with Indonesia. Indonesia's intelligence penetration of Timor was such that by August 1975, when Fretilin defeated UDT in a brief civil war, Indonesian agents were quickly able to recruit the remnants of UDT and other parties and to reassemble them across the border in Indonesian Timor into an invasion force which soon began pushing back into East Timor, along with thinly disguised Indonesian regular troops.

This invasion, encountering particularly difficult terrain, had made relatively little progress by 28 November 1975, when Fretilin formally declared the independence of the Democratic Republic of East Timor. To forestall recognition by the rest of the world, Indonesian forces mounted an open attack on the capital, Dili, on 7 December, and soon extended their control to all major centres. Many thousands of Timorese, both civilians and members of the Fretilin armed forces, died in the attack and subsequent pacification operations. Under Indonesian auspices, UDT, Apodeti and other anti-Fretilin groups formed a provisional government, but this lasted only until 31 May 1976, when a 'People's Representative Council' assembled by the Indonesian forces formally requested integration into Indonesia.

The annexation averted the perceived danger for Indonesia that an economically weak but politically radical small state in the heart of eastern Indonesia would become a base for subversion, but in other respects the Timor operation was a major setback for Indonesia. Timorese resistance did not crumble at the first encounter with the modern Indonesian armed forces, and Timorese civilians did not quickly reconcile themselves to what Indonesia presented as the new political realities. Instead, systematic violence by Indonesian forces attempting to suppress the unexpected resistance hardened the alienation of the East Timorese, and guerrilla resistance quickly consolidated in the countryside, while the new rulers encountered sullen non-cooperation in the towns. It took a series of major military operations between 1977 and 1979, including the resettlement of a large part of the population into supervised strategic hamlets, to establish relative control by the Indonesians in most of the province, and this was achieved only at the cost of major disruptions to agricultural production as a result of which tens of thousands died of starvation.

The international consequences were also serious for Indonesia. Indonesia's good standing as a member of the United Nations was damaged by its refusal to accept Security Council resolutions in late 1975 and early 1976 instructing it to withdraw from the territory, and by its disregard for General Assembly resolutions, passed annually until 1982, condemning its actions. With Fretilin resistance continuing, even after 1979, the former Portuguese colonies of Mozambique and Guinea-Bissau kept the issue alive in Third World forums, thwarting for a decade and a half Suharto's ambition to chair the Non-Aligned Movement. Vocal communities of East Timorese refugees and their supporters in the West have kept the issue alive in many Western countries and have urged those governments to limit their economic cooperation with Indonesia until the issue is resolved. Indonesia has never publicly considered withdrawing from East Timor, but the affair reinforced for Suharto the message from Malari, that is that a mere combination of political repression and imaginative political manipulation was not sufficient to keep his subjects tranquil.

The seriousness of the political problem highlighted by Malari and underlined by East Timor was exacerbated by economic difficulties. Until 1974 New Order Indonesia rode high on a resources boom fuelled especially by oil and timber exports. The oil enterprise was controlled by a state oil company, Pertamina, headed by Ibnu Sutowo, a long-time associate of Suharto. Pertamina did not engage directly in oil production, but rather benefited from production-sharing agreements with foreign oil companies, and the oil which Indonesia thus acquired played a major role in funding the development projects which were central to the New Order's programme. Logging concessions were more widely distributed amongst the friends and associates of the New Order. Here too, however, the Indonesian concession-holders generally played little part in production, but rather allowed outside firms

– initially American, later Japanese and Korean – to log the concessions in exchange for a fee or a share of the proceeds. Oil and timber money softened the direct social impact of the corruption in elite circles: with large sums of money flowing into the economy from outside, the widespread practice of skimming off a percentage of contract prices in commissions and other kickbacks appeared to be a matter of profiting from foreign investors, rather than defrauding the state or robbing the public. A large part, more than half by official estimates, of the armed forces budget came from quasi-private business operations attached to individual units or to the military as a whole,[3] and thus appeared to be a much lesser burden on the treasury than would otherwise have been the case.

In 1975 internal weaknesses in this system caused a major crisis. On the strength of future profits, Pertamina had borrowed hundreds of millions of dollars to finance a portfolio of investments in non-oil ventures ranging from fertiliser and liquefied natural gas production to supertankers, a steel mill and an airline. By late 1974, however, rising oil prices had generated a recession in the West and a consequent tightening of credit. Pertamina, used to rolling over and extending its loans, suddenly found that it was unable to service its debts. Later investigation revealed that the company owed over ten billion dollars at the beginning of 1975. Pertamina was on the verge of bankruptcy and if it collapsed it threatened to take the New Order with it.

In early 1976 Suharto dismissed Ibnu Sutowo and called in the technocrats to mount a rescue operation. Careful management of the debts, a major scaling down of Pertamina's non-oil operations and a series of court cases brought the company's obligations back to manageable proportions by 1977. The oil industry in Indonesia, however, never returned to its previous buoyancy. Not only were foreign investors chastened, but China began to displace Indonesia in the crucial Japanese market. Oil remained a pillar of the economy, but Indonesia's rulers could no longer rely on its revenues to buy the country out of trouble by funding costly development projects and paying off an increasingly avaricious elite. The Pertamina affair provided another proof of the New Order's vulnerability and of the need for a sounder political format.

3. Crouch H 1978 *The Army and Politics in Indonesia* (Cornell University Press, Ithaca), p. 274.

THE NEW INTERPRETATION OF THE PANCASILA

The clearest sign of this new political format was the increased prominence given to the Pancasila after 1974. Before 1974, the Pancasila had been a vague, cover-all slogan whose chief message was that no ideology was to be permitted to dominate Indonesia. In 1974, however, Suharto established a commission to turn the Pancasila into a practical guide for life and politics in Indonesia. In 1978 the MPR formally determined that the Pancasila should be the sole guiding principle for social and political activity in Indonesia. An intensive programme began to train government officials at all levels in the details and implications of the Pancasila, and a programme called Pancasila Moral Education was made compulsory at all levels of the education system. In 1985 the government implemented the MPR's 1978 adoption of the Pancasila by requiring all 'mass organisations', that is, all associations of any kind, including religious organisations, scouts and hobby clubs, to adopt the Pancasila as their 'sole guiding principle' (*azas tunggal*).

The intellectual challenge involved in turning a formula deliberately created to be vague into a set of specific admonitions was achieved by using the individual principles to qualify each other. Thus, for instance, the principle of nationalism was set against the principle of popular sovereignty to produce the proposition that the Pancasila did not permit adversarial politics based on class, race or other social divisions. The principle of belief in God was placed alongside that of social justice to produce the proposition that a just order should not be judged purely in secular or humanist terms. This explication was not presented as fresh thought, but rather as an amplification of the Pancasila as it already existed as a deep-rooted national philosophy. The New Order was particularly keen to downplay Sukarno's authorship of the original five principles, even to the extent of questioning in 1981 whether Sukarno had been responsible for their first formulation in 1945.

Viewed from outside, the Pancasila became an ideology of corporatism. Although the ideological spadework involved in making the Pancasila coherent was the work of a commission, the vision behind it was Suharto's. It presented an idealised vision of Indonesia as a community of diverse social groups all working in harmony for the common good. The new Pancasila denied that there could be any true conflict of interest between different sections of Indonesian society because the greater interest of all society as a whole was the true interest of all its components. And although the original Pancasila did not mention leadership, the amplified version left responsibility for interpreting the national interest firmly with the government in general and the president in particular. It gave scope to Suharto's growing inclination to interpret Indonesia in terms of an idealised traditional Javanese kingdom. Dim popular memories, the enthusiastic myth-making of nationalist leaders and the diligent, romantic reconstructions of Dutch orientalists had combined to give the old Javanese kingdoms an aura of power, prosperity, harmony and happiness which Suharto now sought to reconstruct in modern Indonesia, casting himself in the role of king.

Just how far-reaching this change in the official interpretation of the Pancasila had gone became clear in 1980, when Suharto delivered an informal address to a group of marines at a base near Jakarta. In a passionate address, he denounced Marxism, socialism, nationalism and religion as 'value systems of the past' incompatible with the true identity of the Indonesian people. The Pancasila, created as an umbrella for all ideologies, had become a means of excluding them.

Beneath the banner of the Pancasila, the New Order began a comprehensive campaign to ensure that Indonesians understood their proper place in society. Students were informed without ambiguity that their task was to study and to acquire skills which might later be useful for development. Women were instructed that their primary role was as wives and mothers, sustaining their husbands in work and bringing up their children to be good citizens. Workers in the growing industrial sector were told that they should pursue claims on their employers through what were called 'Pancasila industrial relations', which emphasised the paternal role of employers in deciding what were appropriate conditions and wages for workers, and which tolerated strikes only under the most unusual circumstances.

This emphasis on keeping one's proper place in society reflects what little we know of Suharto's enigmatic personality. No one who knows him well has written anything other than a bland description of his character,[4] and for the most part he is undemonstrative in public, while giving the world few glimpses of his private life. His

---

4. Two English-language biographies which fall into this anodyne category are Roeder O G 1969 *The Smiling General* (Gunung Agung, Jakarta) and Wilson D 1989 *The Long Journey from Turmoil to Self-sufficiency* (Yayasan Persada Nusantara, Jakarta).

autobiography and occasional public outbursts, however, hint at a man for whom duty and a sense of office are important before all else. He has lived almost all his life in official institutions, and it is as if he has allowed his personality to be governed by his official position. As president he has seen his duty as being to deliver political stability and economic development to his country, and his success in both those tasks underpins his generally serene self-assurance and his calm disposal of those who have either stood in his way or outlived their usefulness to him. He evidently sees both honours and access to wealth as a natural reward for holding power, but he is angered by those who use their official position to develop a cult of personality and by those who disregard his achievements to focus on what he considers to be peripheral issues, such as individual human rights or the activities of his family, whose members he also defends fiercely out of a sense of paternal duty.

As well as imbuing the Indonesian public with the ideals of the Pancasila, Suharto's new corporate Indonesian state laid great emphasis on the role of the state bureaucracies, military and civilian. One of the central philosophical tenets of the corporate state was that it was the task of the government to govern, and that it should do so free of external influences. Enforcing the principle of monoloyalty in the civil service was thus not simply a matter of cutting the political parties off from an important source of support; it was meant to insulate the civil service from sectional political demands. The compulsory civil service association, Korpri, was redefined not simply as a rather docile labour union, but as the exclusive social, cultural and political association for government officials, so that officials would have no need for more than casual social contacts outside the civil service. To ensure that this isolation extended to the families of government officials, the government established a parallel organisation called Dharma Wanita (literally the Duty of Women) as an all-encompassing social, cultural and political organisation for the wives of officials. To ensure that neither Korpri nor Dharma Wanita might become a source of indiscipline within the administration, the hierarchy of each organisation exactly parallelled that of the government, with the head of each government section leading the relevant Korpri branch and his wife leading the corresponding Dharma Wanita.[5]

5. No provision was made for the husbands of government officials.

In order to infuse the power of the civil service with a sense of responsibility, the New Order has sought to revitalise *priyayi* culture, the culture of the traditional Javanese administrative elite. Most important has been the strengthening of hierarchical command, so that each official exercises power in an awareness that he or she is being supervised. But the New Order has also revived the aphorisms of traditional *priyayi* rule, stressing, for instance, the motto of the Department of Education and Culture, the ancient injunction *Tut wuri handayani* ('giving inspiration from behind').

This creation of a separate administrative caste and ethos had begun earlier and gone further in the armed forces. Military hierarchy and discipline tends to separate soldiers from civilians in most societies, but the Indonesian armed forces' determination to maintain this separation was reinforced by the experience of the 1940s and 1950s, when military discipline had been weakened by civilian political and economic ties with individual units and commanders. One of the most striking achievements of the Indonesian military since 1950 has been the gradual demilitarisation of civilian society. At the end of 1945, Indonesia had a citizenry in arms, and the military was only one of a number of groups able to wield armed force. During the rationalisations and military actions of the 1950s and 1960s, the volume of firearms available to non-military Indonesians was steadily diminished. At the same time, there has been no conscription and no civilian reserve to provide a reservoir of military experience in civilian society, while recruitment to the armed forces has tended to decline as military authorities have sought to create a more compact and better-trained force. Even crimes of violence in civilian society tend to be committed with knives rather than firearms. The creation of Dharma Pertiwi as a military counterpart to Dharma Wanita was simply a further step in consolidating the social isolation of the armed forces.

In addition to inculcating values by means of slogans and pledges, the military has defined its position by an imaginative recourse to history. Drawing especially on historical interpretations first presented by Nasution,[6] the army presented itself as a national institution with origins independent of the state itself. According

---

6. The most influential of his works, *Tentara Nasional Indonesia* (1963. 2nd edn, 3 vols; Ganaco, Bandung) was written in the early 1950s when Nasution was suspended from his post as army chief of staff for alleged indiscipline as a consequence of the October 1952 affair.

to military mythology, the army sprang into existence in 1945 by the collective endeavour of its officer corps and in the face of obstruction by civilian politicians. Throughout the war of independence, moreover, it provided the key bulwark against the returning Dutch, while during the dark days of the Dutch attack in December 1948, when the civilian cabinet had surrendered, only the army stood between Indonesian independence and defeat at the hands of latter-day colonialism. This myth ignored the massive contribution of civilians to the war of independence and to the construction of the armed forces, as well as glossing over the army's rather patchy performance in the field, but it held enough truth to underpin an increasingly unassailable army view that it had a special right and duty to oversee the affairs of the civilian state. This right and duty came to be summed up by the Sanskrit–Dutch hybrid term *dwifungsi*, or dual function.

Dwifungsi was reinforced from the 1950s by a defence doctrine known as *hankamrata*,[7] which argued that Indonesia would never have the resources to repel an enemy offshore and would therefore have to defend the nation on its own territory. Under these circumstances, the doctrine postulated, the relationship between the armed forces and the people would have a decisive influence on the outcome. Specifically, if the armed forces could rely on popular support, then they could conduct a guerrilla war which an invader would never defeat. *Hankamrata*, therefore, obliged the armed forces not simply to maintain a technical military excellence but to maintain close links with the Indonesian people in order to ensure their loyalty to and cooperation with the defence effort. This doctrine never implied that the people would fight alongside the armed forces in national defence, but simply that the resources of the population would be at the direct disposal of the armed forces. From a purely defence point of view, therefore, the armed forces had a duty to ensure that the state was capable of providing them with logistical and political support, and that the military was in day-to-day contact with the life of the masses.

The practical consequences of *dwifungsi* had been evident well before the New Order came to power. Military officers had participated in administration since 1957, and the armed forces had been directly represented in parliament since 1960. But under the New Order *dwifungsi* was elevated to the status

7. Pertahanan dan Keamanan Rakyat Semesta, Total People's Defence and Security.

of a central state doctrine, although the principle was defined legislatively only in the Defence Law of 1982. Military personnel were posted throughout the administrative structure in order to strengthen and oversee the performance of the civilian hierarchy, holding posts from cabinet minister and provincial governor down to village head. The corporate character of Suharto's Indonesia, in which authority flowed unambiguously from above through the institutions of the state, was thus reinforced.

Perhaps the most ambitious political programme embarked on by Suharto, however, was the transformation of Golkar from a mere government electoral vehicle into a state-led mass party imbued with the ideology of the Pancasila. The move began in 1983, when Suharto pushed a number of constitutional amendments through the Golkar National Congress. The new provisions opened Golkar for the first time to individual members; previously, Indonesian citizens could be involved in Golkar only as members of organisations affiliated with Golkar. The change staked a Golkar claim over the whole of Indonesian politics. The former three-way division of the electorate between Golkar and the two parties, each with its affiliated mass organisations, had ensured a Golkar victory, but it preserved the notion that the parties represented forces in Indonesian society which merited representation in parliament. By opening Golkar to every citizen, however, and by using the Pancasila to deprive the parties of the basis for an identity distinct from Golkar's, the New Order appeared to be paving the way for a single state party. Golkar's drive for members was spectacularly successful. One Golkar leader announced that the organisation intended to recruit a hundred members in each village, which would have given it a membership of 6.5 million, but by the time the membership drive had slowed in 1987, Golkar chairman General Sudharmono claimed twenty-eight million members, including nine million cadres.[8] In the 1987 election, too, Golkar subtly changed its campaign strategy, putting up more women and young people as candidates to appeal to that section of the population, and achieving in the event nearly 73 per cent of the vote, nearly 8 per cent more than it had received in 1982.

---

8. Suryadinata L 1989 *Military Ascendancy and Political Culture: A Study of Indonesia's Golkar* (Ohio University, Athens; Monographs in International Studies), p. 111.

Although Suharto backed his attempted corporatisation of Indonesian society with the massive resources of the Indonesian state, his reshaping of Indonesian politics met unexpected resistance from groups who regarded him as having betrayed old under-standings. The most articulate critique of the New Order came from a group whose affiliations lay with the politics of the 1950s. The group emerged in 1980, when some fifty former politicians, military officers and other public figures presented a petition to parliament objecting to Suharto's denunciation of nationalism, religion and other ideologies as 'value systems of the past'. The petitioners objected that Suharto had arrogated to himself the right to interpret Indonesian ideology and asserted that he had no right to do so: he was merely the servant or mandatory of the parliament and could neither legally nor morally insist that all other Indonesians follow his vision of the country's identity. The group called on parliament to 'review' his speeches, the term 'review' recalling the terms in which parliament had reviewed the actions of Sukarno when he was being stripped of his powers.

The imposition of a Pancasila-based society was also resisted by religious groups who found insistence on the Pancasila as sole guiding principle directly in conflict with their religious beliefs. Both Muslims and Christians objected with varying degrees of vehemence to the 1984 draft law which formally required adherence to the Pancasila, but the most violent response came on the streets of Tanjung Priok, Jakarta's port area, on 12 September 1984. Tensions were high, because the notionally Islamic party PPP had recently, under heavy state pressure, accepted a law requiring it to adopt the Pancasila as its sole basic principle, thus giving the central principles of Islam secondary status. The incident took place when a large crowd marched on an army post to demand the release of two men detained for allegedly assaulting security officers said to have defiled a prayer house. Alarmed by being confronted by this large and unauthorised display of public opinion, local army units fired into the crowd, killing certainly dozens and possibly hundreds of people; the bodies were removed quickly by the security forces and the exact number of dead is unknown.

Neither the Petition of Fifty nor the Tanjung Priok killings caused a crisis of confidence in the New Order in the way in which the Malari affair had done. The government moved deftly in each case to deal with those it saw as its enemies. Suharto deprived the petitioners of their right to travel abroad, banned the media from mentioning their activities and removed from those with business interests their access to government contracts and permits. Most of the leading figures involved in the Tanjung Priok demonstration died in the shooting, but a distinguished former general and former secretary-general of ASEAN, H.R. Dharsono, who called publicly for an inquiry into the killings and who distributed a version of events differing from the government's bland account, was tried on charges of subversion and sentenced to ten years in jail in late 1985.

The petition and the Tanjung Priok affair symbolised the stripping away of the old New Order coalition from Suharto's government. Most of the petitioners had been significant or powerful figures whose support for the New Order against Sukarno in the mid-1960s had helped bring about the end of Guided Democracy. The Tanjung Priok demonstrators were of a younger generation, but they were heirs to the pious Muslims who gave the New Order coalition its most public popular support. Suharto, however, had discarded them well before they discarded him, and their outrage stemmed in part from their feelings of powerlessness. The petitioners survived both as a more or less coherent forum for discussing the shortcomings of the New Order and as a kind of shorthand for that group in Indonesian society which would like to restore what it sees as the old consensus of Indonesian politics, that is a system which broadly preserves and respects the integrity of the many cultural, social, religious and ideological groups making up Indonesia. Islamic resentment at the continued ascendancy of what radicals see as rampant secularism still festered, too, in the poor districts of Tanjung Priok and elsewhere in Indonesia, but for the moment Suharto's Pancasila state reigned supreme.

CHAPTER TEN
Social Change and Future Prospects

For three decades and more after the declaration of independence in 1945, Indonesian politics was a working out of older tensions and antagonisms, of social, economic, cultural and economic divisions which dated from the colonial era and before. The New Order regime represented an attempt by Suharto – more successful than earlier attempts by Sukarno – to set these divisions to one side in what he interpreted to be the national interest, first by suspending mass politics and later imposing his own view of the essential character of the nation. As Suharto defined it, the Pancasila state combined a goal of sustained and accelerated economic growth, development and prosperity with a deeply conservative political vision which gathered power into the hands of the president and envisaged a meek and obedient public.

The political stability which the New Order created, however, along with the policies of economic development which it energetically pursued, opened new opportunities for social change. Suharto's attempt to reshape Indonesian society in the image of an idealised Javanese kingdom took place in the face of social change on a scale not seen since the massive transformations of the colonial era. Indonesian society today is significantly different from the society which Suharto inherited in 1966, and these changes collectively have meant that Indonesia is moving away from the Pancasila democracy model, at least as it was initially formulated. In this chapter we shall examine some of the more important changes which have taken place and suggest the direction they may be leading. Before we consider these social changes, however, it is necessary to examine two major problems in the New Order's own efforts to implement Pancasila Democracy, problems which

144

seriously undermine the Suharto experiment even without major social change.

PROBLEMS WITH PANCASILA DEMOCRACY

The first of these problems lies in the official efforts to establish Pancasila as the national ideology, efforts which have fundamentally shaped the way politics works in late New Order Indonesia. It is unclear, however, to what extent these attempts to make Pancasila a living ideology for the mass of the Indonesian people have been successful. Most citizens have now received years of education in Pancasila and all government decisions are supposed to be taken within a Pancasila framework, but there is little indication that reference to Pancasila has passed beyond simply being a ritual. Golkar may have recruited millions of members as the political expression of Pancasila, but it is likely that most of those have joined for career reasons, rather than out of conviction.

A major part of the problem here is that Pancasila was created in 1945 as a non-ideology, as a device to suspend the conflict between deeply antagonistic ideologies. This was hardly promising raw material for the construction of a new ideology. More important, the New Order government has tended to stifle what independent life Pancasila might have developed by insisting that only its own interpretation of the five principles is valid. This has given Pancasila an instrumental character, the appearance that it is a convenient tool employed at the discretion of the government and only in the government's own interests. The corporatist ideology which the New Order government has attempted to squeeze out of Pancasila has not been able to take serious account of the notion of individual, class or other group rights within society. Rather than accepting such rights and mediating in the conflicts which would thus arise, it has tended to deny that any such conflicts can exist. The complexity of Indonesia's society and economy makes this an inadequate view and means in turn that the survival of the Suharto model of Pancasila as a political force is highly dependent on the political, social and economic environment in which it is located.

The second problem for Pancasila Democracy is a more fundamental one. Pancasila itself is a very loosely defined, idealistic set principles, ones with which few in Indonesia could possibly take exception. This very lack of shape, this amorphousness, is the great strength of Pancasila. It immediately starts to lose this strength

145

the moment political leaders attempt to put it into effect because political realities hardly ever match political ideals. This is, of course, hardly a problem unique to Pancasila: similar observations could be made about virtually all sets of ideas from Christianity to communism. But it means that as soon as Indonesian leaders are seen by the population as having acted in ways inconsistent with the ideals of Pancasila, their legitimacy and that of the Pancasila political system they lead are brought into question. This has certainly happened as a result of abuses of power committed in the president's name.

The corporatist system proposed by Pancasila gives enormous responsibility to the president and accepts it as reasonable that he should be amply rewarded. Since the early 1980s, however, Suharto's children, especially his three sons, Sigit, Bambang and Hutomo, as well as his daughter Siti, have been energetically using their proximity to the palace to amass fortunes and to build business empires. The children had done well earlier as silent partners in the business operations of Suharto's business associate Liem Sioe Liong, who enjoyed privileged access to government permits and other advantages. Liem was fortunate in enjoying these privileges when the Indonesian economy was a wasteland waiting for reconstruction. The Suharto children, however, began moving into a corporate landscape already well populated with new entrepreneurs nurtured by the developmental policies of the New Order. The special advantage which the children enjoyed in access to government decisions was reason enough for resentment of their activities, but they have proven to be not just competitive but predatory, depriving established firms of their livelihood and forcing business owners to sell profitable operations at a discount. Suharto himself does not appear to be involved in such activities, but his refusal to rein in his family has become a significant complaint against him even amongst groups which are otherwise his strong supporters. More importantly, however, the unbridled activities of the children demonstrate the vulnerability of the New Order, as it is presently constituted, to any future president who may decide to put his own interests ahead of those of the nation. Even Indonesians who see no benefit in untrammelled democracy can see benefits in the checks and balances offered by a greater degree of democracy than presently operates.

The failure of Pancasila Democracy to encompass all Indonesians is also evident in the government's continuing reliance on political repression and political manipulation. The New Order continues to bring a heavy hand down on dissenters, jailing student and Muslim activists on slender grounds. Nor has there been any hint that it will withdraw the massive government backing and restrictive regulations which have ensured a Golkar victory in the last five elections. The government, moreover, has continued to play on public fears of communism and of radical Islam. Sections of the government continue to warn publicly against the 'latent danger' said to be presented by the presumably underground PKI, while unexplained disasters, such as major fires, are often blamed on the communists. During the late 1980s, moreover, the government began to require that Indonesians employed in a wide range of sensitive occupations, not only in government and the military but in education, the media and the law, should be 'environmentally clean' (*bersih lingkungan*). This meant not only that they should have no personal connections with the PKI and the 1965 coup, but that their social environment, including families, friends and associates should be similarly free. In the run-up to the election of the president and vice-president in March 1988, accusations of environmental uncleanliness were directed even at Suharto's chosen vice-presidential candidate, Sudharmono, and a number of other politicians were forced to resign later in the year when incriminating aspects of their pasts were exposed. At the same time, the government has made much of what it calls 'right-wing' challenges, by which it means radical Islam. A number of incidents, such as an outbreak of unrest in the southern Sumatra province of Lampung in 1989, which was apparently instigated by local Muslim leaders, have also been highlighted to reinforce the impression that the New Order prevents Indonesia from being hijacked by any extremist or minority group.

CHANGES IN RURAL SOCIETY

Even more important than the ideological and practical problems in the implementation of Pancasila Democracy, however, are the social changes in Indonesia which have undermined the traditional forms of political authority which Pancasila Democracy has tried to cultivate. Many of the most important of these changes have been in rural society.

Indonesian villages have never been static institutions: change has been a constant part of village life. The New Order period, however, has seen a significant quickening of the pace of change in rural Indonesian society, a function largely of the government's greater willingness to intervene in rural life, and of its greater capacity to do so. The most obvious example of such intervention has been the so-called 'green revolution', which brought wholesale changes in cultivation techniques, in turn producing major social change. The green revolution brought significant increases in rice production, and in earnings for those farmers able to take full benefit of the new farming techniques. But these tended to be limited to the richer farmers, often village officials with access not only to their own land but also to *tanah bengkok*, village land which was assigned to them for their use so long as they held office. Because of the expense involved in participation in the green revolution, poorer farmers, and in particular those with little or no land of their own, were either forced into debt in their struggle to continue farming, or else were forced off their land altogether. Meanwhile land itself became more valuable as a source of wealth, and community-based restraints on its purchase and sale diminished; as a result land was increasingly regarded as a tradeable item which could be bought and sold like any other. People with access to capital – village officials, for instance, and the better-off townspeople – bought up land from the traditional owners, although land ownership remains more dispersed in Indonesia than in any other country in Southeast Asia: holdings of a hundred hectares are not completely unknown, but 'big' landlords in Indonesia still typically own less than twenty hectares. Women suffered particularly heavily, as changing cultivation techniques displaced them from their traditional agricultural roles either by men or by the new machinery coming into widespread use by the 1980s. More people found work outside agriculture, often in rural towns or even the larger cities, access to which was made substantially easier by the transport revolution which saw at least rural Java covered by a web of routes served by small public buses. The increased availability of education for children also contributed to the flow of people out of the village into the towns and cities. On the other hand there was also a movement of people into the villages and to country towns. These people were chiefly the recently-minted professionals of New Order Indonesia: in particular the teachers, doctors and paramedical personnel brought in to staff the village schools and community health centres which had appeared in virtually every village by the late 1980s.

The overall effect of these changes was an increasingly rapid rate of corrosion of the long-standing social and moral ties which bound agricultural communities together. These ties were never egalitarian ones; the New Order certainly did not introduce factors such as landlessness and wage labour to Indonesia's villages, which had known these phenomena for centuries. But even in inequality rural society had been held together by bonds of responsibility and obligation which were backed not so much by wealth as by history. It was these ties which were deteriorating, to be replaced, increasingly, by ties based either on wealth or on connections with the central government.

THE MIDDLE CLASS AND DEMAND FOR DEMOCRACY

These changes in rural society are paralleled by dramatic changes in urban Indonesia. The growing sophistication of business, industry and government has demanded an increasingly skilled workforce at managerial, technical and manual levels. During the last thirty years Indonesia has experienced a boom in education and training unprecedented since the sudden expansion of schooling in the later nineteenth and early twentieth centuries which helped to trigger the growth of nationalism. Vastly higher levels of literacy and increasing exposure to the outside world have combined to create a generation of Indonesians who are less inclined than their parents to take the authority of their rulers for granted. Nearly half the Indonesian population was born after the traumatic events of 1965–66, and for this generation the lessons of the past are inevitably a more muted warning against democracy than for their parents.

In Indonesia, moreover, and indeed throughout much of Southeast Asia, a broad confidence in human progress remains strong. In contrast to the jaded and more sceptical West, the majority of people believe that the human condition can continue to improve. Under these circumstances, the New Order's achievements in economic growth and development contrast sharply with its conservative, even static, approach to political development. The New Order has delivered increased prosperity to many, perhaps most, levels of society, but the disparity in income and living standard between rich and poor has reached a point many Indonesians feel is unsustainable, both morally and practically. Indonesians who found grudgingly acceptable the New Order's ruthlessness in overriding sectional interests in the interests of development are hard put to justify the dispossession of peasant farmers from their lands for luxury projects such as golf courses.[1] There is a significant tendency to see Suharto's New Order, therefore, simply as one stage amongst many in the process of political development in Indonesia, and to accept that the political verities of the last thirty years will be up for negotiation once Suharto departs.

This mood for change is illustrated by the excitement that accompanied talk of increased openness or *keterbukaan* in 1989. *Keterbukaan* was itself a direct translation of the term *glasnost*, used by reformers in the former Soviet Union to signal the move from tight political restriction and control. What *keterbukaan* might mean in the Indonesian context was never entirely clear. At the least – and, some government critics feared, at the most too – *keterbukaan* meant simply a relaxation of political censorship and an apparent willingness on the part of government leaders to open dialogue with community groups. Even this relatively minor development seemed threatened in early 1990; evidently alarmed by the new freedom of discussion, the government closed the window on openness with official reminders of the importance of national discipline and leadership. As we write, it is by no means clear whether this position will prove sustainable in the long run. The initial flush of *keterbukaan* had made it evident that there was a widespread unmet demand for further democratisation present in Indonesian society. 1991 and 1992 saw the emergence of a variety of quasi-political organisations – such as Democracy Forum, Indonesian League for the Restoration of Democracy and the Forum for the Restoration of People's Sovereignty – seeking greater political freedoms. Of at least equal significance was the establishment of the independent trade union Setiakawan – 'Solidarity', in yet another evocative reminder of Eastern Europe. Although the government has made it clear it does not welcome these organisations, and that Setiakawan at least is formally illegal, thus far it has neither banned them nor formally taken action against their leaders or members.

One further factor which may strengthen the pressures for political liberalisation is the emergence of a largely urban middle

1. In 1981, a public opinion poll by the news magazine *Tempo* recorded that more than 50 per cent of respondents regarded 'social disturbances between rich and poor' as the greatest danger to national unity.

class. In Western Europe, North America and Australia, the emergence of such a class gave impetus to the political developments which saw the beginnings of modern Western political democracy. Some observers have suggested the same process will take place in Indonesia. This argument by analogy, though, may not be an powerful as it at first appears. The Indonesian middle class is very much the beneficiary of the New Order state: its members have reaped the rewards of the economic development and relative political stability Indonesia has enjoyed since the early 1970s. They are not likely to be interested in giving support to movements or leaders whose actions endanger that development and stability. For the foreseeable future, they are likely to be satisfied with the kinds of relatively minor concessions towards political liberalisation represented by *keterbukaan*. In the economic arena, they are also likely to want to see a continuation of current policies, rather than seeking any vastly different ones. It is extremely unlikely, for instance, that there will be any significant push for economic policies which are more equitable or seek to close the yawning gap between rich and poor. Nevertheless, the middle class seems by now to have become a permanent part of the Indonesian political landscape and thus one with which future Indonesian governments will have to contend.

As we write in the early 1990s the Suharto government appears to be moving towards seeing its role as one of mediating between this wider range of political interests, rather than imposing a single orthodoxy. The corporatist interpretation of Pancasila thus seems to be declining in importance in the New Order's political strategy, though it is too early to say how far or how fast this change will proceed.

CHANGING MILITARY DOCTRINE

If, however, change is expected after Suharto's departure, there is no certainty about where it will lead. One of the most important determining elements is likely to be the attitude of the military. President Suharto came to power by virtue of the military power he commanded, and the Indonesian armed forces remain the central pillar of the New Order regime. They not only guarantee the New Order against violent overthrow but as a result of *dwifungsi* they give the civil apparatus of state an extra resilience and discipline. *Dwifungsi* has been enshrined in law and, as we have seen,

151

is supported by powerful historical myths. Significant political change in Indonesia will depend on a revision or removal of the notion of *dwifungsi*. And of the two possibilities, the former is much the more likely, for a variety of reasons.

First, the practical value of *dwifungsi* to the governance of the state is probably less today than it has ever been since the doctrine was first enunciated. In the late 1950s, it could well be argued that without the participation of the army in national and regional administration, the state would have disintegrated. The civil apparatus of the Indonesian state was simply unable to carry out its assigned functions with even minimal levels of efficiency. That civil apparatus is now however relatively competent and well-trained. A gradual withdrawal of the military from administration is unlikely to bring about a significant deterioration in performance. Indeed, the number of military personnel in civilian posts has already shown a tendency to decline.

Second, despite the official emphasis on people-based defence, the policies of the New Order have tended to transform the military into a distinct caste, enjoying an official status higher than civilians, dominated by its own rituals and confined to its own social world. Today's Indonesian soldiers, in some respects at least, share less of the world view of the people they are instructed to defend than did their predecessors drawn directly out of society into the revolutionary army which fought the Dutch, and this militates against the symbiotic relationship which the official doctrine of 'total people's defence and security' envisages. Greater national wealth, moreover, has given the armed forces access to more advanced technology, and has encouraged a tendency to rely on technical superiority rather than mass support.

Third, and perhaps most important of all, there is evidence that sections of the younger generation of military officers who did not experience the struggle against the Dutch see *dwifungsi*, the military involvement in politics and government, in a rather different light from their seniors. They see it as directly undermining the armed forces' defence task. They resent the diversion of trained army officers from military matters into civil administration, and they see danger in the fact that the armed forces' political involvement continues to leave them open to political influence. This danger is particularly serious because close engagement in politics wins the armed forces more enemies than friends. It has been reported that sections of the Indonesian army see the military's poor performance in East Timor as a consequence of its heavy engagement in national politics.

Two major barriers exist to the military's abdication from power. First is the military's own uncertainty whether the nation could survive without it. Today's senior officers were trained into a belief that civilian politicians cannot be trusted to pursue the national interest; nearly three decades of tight military control on politics has done little to give potential civilian successors the political skills needed to operate in a more open environment. Concern that a military withdrawal from politics may lead to political chaos is a powerful disincentive for change. Second, the military has many interests which would be at some risk if they were to loosen their grip on power. With a vast range of career options and lucrative business and administrative opportunities available to officers on their retirement, the Indonesian officer corps has a good deal to lose if *dwifungsi* is abandoned altogether.

From the military's point of view, the most satisfactory means of withdrawal would be by way of an orderly handover to like-minded civilian administrators, with the military remaining in the background as guarantors of the political order. The case for a gradual civilianisation of the administration is underpinned by the New Order's spectacular successes in the economic sphere. Even the dramatic decline in oil and gas prices during the 1980s has been partly offset by effective policies to increase exports of textiles, timber products, processed natural rubber, cement, electrical appliances, fish and other products; the state treasury, too, has diversified its sources of revenue, becoming steadily less dependent on oil and gas. This contrasts sharply with the comparable collapse of rubber prices in 1951, after the Korean War boom. Indonesia's economic managers at that time were unable to cope with the sudden drop in income, and the price collapse marked the beginning of the long political and economic unravelling of parliamentary democracy. A key element in all of this, though, will be preservation of the business interests of the military. Given that the military is dependent for much of its funds on its commercial enterprises, receiving only a relatively small proportion of the money it needs from the state budget, any threat to those enterprises would directly threaten the capacity of the military to continue to buy, maintain and operate the sophisticated equipment on which it has come increasingly to rely. Moreover, today's senior officers and NCOs are tomorrow's retirees, who will be expecting to be able to supplement their pensions with employment in military-connected businesses.

The civilian administrators are hampered, however, by a pervasive reputation for corruption. Corrupt practices, ranging from soliciting and accepting bribes and misusing confidential government information to the simple collection of wages without turning up for work, became widespread during the Japanese occupation and have never been seriously tackled under any of the political systems of independent Indonesia. Periodic drives against low-level corruption have occurred, and occasionally more senior figures have been made a modest example of, but corrupt habits remain deeply entrenched in sections of the bureaucracy, where they diminish both the performance and the reputation of the administration. Nonetheless, aside from the generally ineffective process of criminal investigation, three strategies against corruption have been pursued with some success. First, the salaries of government officials have been gradually increased in order to diminish the need for corrupt behaviour. Second, technical training has been improved in order to raise levels of professionalism within the administration, so that corrupt practices will be seen as illegitimate. And third, the government has reduced some opportunities for corruption by simplifying government procedures. The most spectacular such case occurred in 1985, when the government sent the inspectors of the notoriously corrupt Customs service home on full salary and contracted a Swiss firm, the Societé Générale de Surveillance, to undertake customs inspections on its behalf. The precise extent to which such measures have actually diminished the level of overall corruption, however, is impossible to say.

A further political liability for the civilian administration, paradoxically, is Indonesia's strong tradition of state intervention in the economy. This tradition arose both out of strong socialist influences in the nationalist movement and out of the antagonism which many politicians and bureaucrats felt towards Western and Chinese firms operating in Indonesia; it was reflected in nationalisation of businesses and in the spinning of a tight web of regulations and restrictions intended to ensure that capitalist enterprise did not exploit the Indonesian people. This tight net of regulation was amongst the factors enabling the entrenchment of corruption in the civilian administration. Corruption, however, allowed a few favoured operators in each political era to slip through the regulations and to flourish on the basis of special treatment, including soft loans, easy government permits, privileged access to government permits and state-protected monopolies. During the 1950s and 1960s, the rapidly changing political order meant that most of the favoured businessmen enjoyed only a brief period of privilege before being cast aside. With nearly three decades of relative stability since 1965, however, a significant number of Indonesian businessmen have been able to build business empires so extensive and so well capitalised that they are no longer dependent on government favour.

This new business elite includes members of Suharto's own family, as well as current and past close associates. Liem Sioe Liong, Suharto's business associate, is said to be one of the world's ten richest bankers, and controls a network of enterprises including cement manufacture, flour-milling and many other activities. Ibnu Sutowo, former head of Pertamina, retains an empire of trading, manufacturing and financial concerns. Many of these business people continue to receive patronage from the presidential palace, but they find their economic activity hampered rather than helped by the maze of government regulations and controls. Less well-connected businessmen, too, have come to flourish under the stability and prosperity of the New Order, and from all these groups have come increasingly strong arguments for government policies more sympathetic to business in general, and especially for deregulation of the economy. Such arguments would have been dismissed once as business promoting its own self-interest, but with the decline in oil revenue, the Indonesian government increasingly needs a prosperous and efficient private sector as part of its domestic tax base. Perhaps the clearest sign of this reorientation is the 1987 law reorganising the national Chamber of Commerce and Industry, in which the principle of profit-making was for the first time formally recognised as legitimate.[2]

Ironically, sections of the bureaucracy have adopted environmental protection as a platform for resisting such arguments. Indonesia inherited from the Dutch little legal or administrative infrastructure for protecting the environment and until the mid-1970s made few efforts in areas such as nature conservation or pollution control. From the mid 1970s, however, the technocrats became increasingly aware of the long-term problems which neglect of environmental issues might cause for Indonesia, and

2. Macintyre A J 1991 *Business and Politics in Indonesia* (Allen & Unwin, Sydney; Asian Studies Association of Australia, Southeast Asian Publications Series), p. 55.

they began a gradual change in policy. A major programme to establish national parks and other protected areas was initiated, and training programmes were begun at many universities to equip future administrators and technical specialists with an appreciation of environmental issues. In 1990 a set of tough new regulations on pollution came into effect. These regulations and their implementation have met at times stiff resistance from affected businesses, from sections of the administration and even from the Indonesian public – farmers removed from their lands to create buffer zones around national parks have been understandably hostile to the idea – and they have been far from universally implemented. They represent, however, a major new effort by sections of the bureaucracy to stake out legitimate grounds for continued regulation. The massive growth of the Jakarta–Bogor–Tanggerang–Bekasi conurbation, the population of which is expected to reach twenty-five million by the year 2000,[3] can similarly be expected to bring new demands for tighter urban planning in the interest of all the city's residents.   In short, the arguments over environmental protection and planning not only give the administration a new platform from which to argue that bureaucratic control is in the national interest. The success of these arguments, in turn, is likely to have an important effect on the bureaucracy's ability to present itself as a credible manager of the country without military backing.

THE RISE OF ISLAM

In contemplating the possibility of greater democracy in Indonesia, one of the main uncertainties is the role which will be played by Islam, whose strength currently seems to be growing. When nationalism first became a force in colonial Indonesia, it seemed that Islam, as the religion of the great majority, would be a natural vehicle for the political aspirations of the Indonesian people. This did not happen, for two broad reasons. First, as we have seen, nationalists placed such a high priority on unity that they were reluctant to alienate the followers of Kejawen and the significant

3. For a recent overview of the present and potential problems faced by Jakarta, see Castles L 1989 Jakarta: Piling Detroit onto New York and Washington? In Hill H and Mackie J A C (eds) *Indonesia Assessment 1988* (Australian National University, Research School of Pacific Studies, Canberra), pp. 49–52.

non-Muslim minorities by allowing their vision of Indonesia to have an Islamic flavour. And second, Muslims themselves, even orthodox Muslims, were often willing to concede political power to secular forces in exchange for support and protection of their religious observance. In the colonial period, a great many Muslims postponed indefinitely the struggle for an Islamic state and concentrated instead on paying proper respect to Allah and on the slow task of creating a more Islamic society. Thus, when the Indonesian state was formed, Islam was not recognised as the national religion, and moves by some Muslim political leaders to have the constitution require all Muslims to follow Islamic law were defeated. During the 1950s and 1960s the Muslim parties were never strong enough or united enough in parliament or at election time to impose their vision on the rest of Indonesia.[4] Under the New Order, political restriction and control, especially the funnelling of Muslim political activity into the artificial and deeply divided PPP, made it clear to Muslims that the chance of achieving their aims through legal political channels were minimal.

Some Muslims concluded under these circumstances that the only way forward was armed revolution, and in the early 1980s revolutionary groups with names such as Komando Jihad (Holy War Command) launched a number of attacks on symbolic targets: churches, a Chinese-owned bank, the headquarters of the national radio and television and the ancient Buddhist monument of Borobudur in Central Java (reconstruction and refurbishment of which had just been completed as a joint project between the Indonesian government and UNESCO). They also gained wide publicity for attacking a police station in West Java and hijacking an aircraft.

A much greater proportion of the pious Muslim population, however, concluded that the political struggle could not be won and that their efforts should be devoted to society as a whole. In December 1984 this process reached a landmark when the Nahdatul Ulama decided to withdraw from the PPP. This decision was prompted by a law specifically requiring the parties to adopt Pancasila as their sole guiding principle, which meant in effect that the PPP would no longer be even nominally a Muslim party, but it reflected a broader NU conclusion that party politics had become

4. In the 1955 general elections, the three major Muslim political parties – Masjumi, NU and PSII – together cornered a total of 42 per cent of the vote; potentially enough for them to have formed a very powerful Islamic bloc in the parliament. In fact such a bloc was never formed.

futile. The same process has seen numerous Islamic leaders join Golkar, not out of any affection for its principles but out of a calculation that they can pursue their religious aims better within, and with the support of the state.

Paradoxically, a consequence of this thoroughgoing depoliticisation of Islam has been a growing Islamisation of Indonesian society, especially at the expense of Kejawen. Shorn of their former political implications, the public aspects of Islamic observance, including fasting during Ramadhan, praying five times a day and making the pilgrimage to Mecca, are now a sign of respectable piety, not potential subversion. In the Javanese countryside, moreover, Muslim teachers, often members of Golkar, have been inculcating more orthodox Islamic principles into the children of the followers of Kejawen, encouraging them to see the old mystical practices as undesirable and primitive superstition. Many observers still see enormous resilience in the Kejawen traditions of rural Java, and the New Order government has set out to shore up the influence of Kejawen by giving it government sponsorship through the Department of Education and Culture and by arguing that the constitution specifically distinguishes and recognises both religion and belief.[5] The long-term probability, however, is that these traditions will become an increasingly marginal relic of the past in Indonesian society, as has happened in Iran, Afghanistan and elsewhere. If this is so, governments after that of Suharto will be faced with an Indonesian society vastly more Islamic than in the past.

The growing significance of Islam has been apparent in the increasing vehemence with which Muslims have pursued limited, basically religious goals, such as the abolition of gambling, especially state sponsored lotteries and football pools, and the gaining of permission for Muslim girls to wear the Muslim headdress, or *jilbab*, to school, even though it was not a part of the official school uniform. In the run-up to the 1992 general elections, in fact, Suharto seemed at times to be deliberately cultivating Muslim groups as significant arbiters of public opinion.

5. The relevant section of the constitution refers initially simply to religion (*agama*) but subsequently to religion and belief (*agama dan kepercayaan*). Under the Old Order, a narrow interpretation of this clause gave formal recognition only to the five major world religions: Islam, Catholicism, Protestantism, Hinduism and Buddhism. The New Order's more liberal interpretation could allow the followers of Kejawen to be counted separately and not as part of the Muslim community. This would significantly reduce the numerical strength of Islam in Indonesia, and is seen by many Muslims as infringing Islamic law, which prohibits apostasy, or conversion to another religion.

Closer adherence to Islam, however, does not necessarily mean that Indonesia will come to resemble the Muslim states of the Middle East in the political power of traditionalist Islamic scholars. Although Indonesian Islam has been strongly influenced in the past by currents of thought from the Middle East, Indonesia itself is the intellectual centre of a major new school of Islamic thought which has been called Neo-Modernism. The Neo-Modernists depart from traditional and even conventional Modernist Islam in regarding most of the social practices associated with Islam – polygamy, seclusion of women, the prohibition on lending money at interest and so on – as human interpretations not Divine will. They insist that the Qur'an and the Hadith (the recorded sayings of the Prophet Muhammad) are the only reliable guide to Allah's intentions and that these sources lay down fundamental principles of submission to God, social justice and equality, not specific rules of behaviour. They see practices such as the seclusion of women as an appropriate application of Divine principles to the conditions in 7th century Arabia, but argue that what was appropriate then may not be correct now. The most important Neo-Modernist thinker, Nurcholish Madjid, describes this process of taking Divine sanction away from practices which are not entitled to it as 'desacralisation'.

The significance of Neo-Modernist thought is two-fold. First, it strips away from Islam social practices which many people, inside and outside Islam, find barbarous or primitive, and thus makes it possible to be both thoroughly Muslim and thoroughly modern. And second, it sharply diminishes the religious authority of Islamic scholars by focusing belief on a relatively small volume of sacred texts, rather than on the vast mass of religious commentary which appeared in the centuries after Muhammad. This makes religious knowledge accessible to all believers as individuals and as members of the Muslim community. It thus restores to Islam the practical equality of all believers which was one of its early characteristics and which was obscured in later centuries by the rising authority of religious scholars. This religious commitment to practical equality in turn lays a firm basis for democratic politics.

Neo-Modernism, moreover, is not merely the brainchild of isolated Muslim thinkers; it has become the dominant stream of thought in the influential Muslim Students Association (Himpunan Mahasiswa Islam, HMI) and has a wide though still minority following in the Indonesian Muslim community in general, to an extent unparalleled in the rest of the Muslim world. If, as seems likely, a greater degree of democratisation follows the eventual departure of Suharto from Indonesian politics, Islamic Neo-Modernism is in a position to become a major political and intellectual force.

ETHNICITY AND REGIONAL POLITICS

One final area of uncertainty in Indonesia's future is the relationship between central authority and the outlying regions. The strength of Indonesian nationalism in unifying the diverse ethnic groups of the archipelago has always been impressive. In the immediate aftermath of decolonisation, only the Republic of the South Moluccas emerged as a serious attempt by one ethnic group to secede from the new state. The other great struggles of Indonesian politics – the Darul Islam rebellion, the PRRI–Permesta uprising and the political tensions leading to the massacres of 1965–66 – were all to do with the identity of Indonesia as a whole, not with efforts to leave Indonesia.

Indonesian nationalism owes its power to many factors. It emerged as an appealing alternative to, and a means of overcoming, colonial rule and its tired indigenous agents; the national language, Indonesian, is derived from Malay, the language of a minor ethnic group from the coasts of Sumatra, and so has saved Indonesia from the destructive effects of a struggle over the status of the majority language, Javanese. Even the fact that the Dutch happened to establish their administrative centre on the northwest coast of Java, well away from the ethnic Javanese regions of Central and East Java, has contributed to Jakarta's acceptability as a national capital. To an important extent, moreover, the idea of Indonesia has been powerful because it has seemed to suggest modernity and opportunity, symbolised by the flexible and rapidly evolving Indonesian language, by a dynamic national music culture, by economic opportunities and by the stature which came from participating in the world's fifth (now fourth) largest country.

That the solvent power of the idea of Indonesia is limited, however, is indicated by the experiences of provinces or ethnic groups which have struggled either to maintain their specific identity within the Indonesian state, or to pull out of the state altogether. Such struggles have taken place in Irian Jaya, East Timor and Aceh, in all of which there are today armed insurgency movements challenging rule from Jakarta, with varying degrees of success and popular support. In Irian Jaya, resistance is spearheaded by the Free Papua Movement (Organisasi Papua Merdeka, OPM); in East Timor by the East Timor National Liberation Front (Fretilin). In both cases, the formal objective of the struggle is independence from Indonesia. In Aceh, opposition to Jakarta's rule initially worked through the Darul Islam, which aimed not for Acehnese independence but rather for the transformation of Indonesia into an Islamic state. Since at least the 1970s, though, this opposition has taken on a different character under the direction of the Free Aceh Movement (Gerakan Aceh Merdeka) which, as its name suggests, seeks Acehnese independence from Indonesia. None of these armed resistance movements has succeeded in establishing significant liberated zones, let alone in approaching full military success, but each of them remains the armed expression of what appears to be, at least in the cases of Irian Jaya and East Timor, a much wider civilian antagonism to New Order rule.

Opposition to Jakarta is partly a product of history. As we described in earlier chapters, Irian Jaya had been separated artificially from the Netherlands Indies by the Dutch in 1949 and was developed as a separate colony until 1963, when Indonesian and international pressure finally forced the Dutch to return it to Indonesia. East Timor, which had never been part of the Netherlands Indies,[6] was invaded and annexed by Indonesia in 1975–76 to forestall the possible establishment of an independent left-wing government. Aceh had been an independent state until 1870, when it was attacked by the Dutch, but it was not even largely pacified until 1914 and was quick to throw off Dutch rule in the 1940s. In Irian Jaya and East Timor, nationalism is also a consequence of deliberate anti-Indonesian campaigning by both colonial powers before the Indonesian takeover, which led local people to expect the worst. And to a significant degree it is a consequence of the bitter fact that many of the dire Dutch and Portuguese predictions came true (as we outlined in Chapters 8 and 9), and continue to come true; as recently as November 1991, Indonesian troops killed at least fifty unarmed demonstrators in a cemetery in Dili. All these factors have created a sense of alienation

---

6. The border between Dutch and Portuguese territory in the Timor region was formally demarcated by treaty in 1859 and partitioned an area in which Dutch and Portuguese influence had been strongly intertwined.

from Indonesia which may last for generations. Aceh has not experienced the same kind of separation from the Indonesian state, although ruthless suppression of the Aceh Movement may be creating the same sense of historical grievance.

These nationalisms are also a consequence of the fact that the people they represent feel left out of the idea of Indonesia as it is now officially maintained. Indonesia in the 1990s claims to have made its decisions about national identity and it offers its constituent ethnic groups no special forum in which to debate the issue and indeed no right to say otherwise. For most of Indonesia's peoples, the ones who have clearly been absorbed into the mainstream of national life, this situation presents no problems. But for those such as the Irianese, East Timorese and many Acehnese, for whom the sense of regional or ethnic identity is still very strong, the costs of accepting the status quo are much higher. Indonesia's political order is a product of its tangled history since independence and regions which did not participate in that history are less enthusiastic about accepting it.

It has been customary to see regionalism in Indonesia as a phenomenon of the past, an atavistic sentiment which is being steadily eroded by modernity. The recent break-up of the Soviet Union, the close-to-complete partition of Belgium and the strength of the secessionist movements in the United Kingdom, Spain and Canada, however, demonstrate that regionalism is not necessarily a primitive phenomenon; rather it can be instead a tool for reorienting regions towards new centres of power. The Scottish campaign for 'independence within Europe' is perhaps the clearest instance of this. None of the three provinces concerned gains a great deal economically from its connection with Indonesia. To be sure, Irian Jaya and East Timor receive a significant proportion of the aid Indonesia receives from abroad, but both would presumably be eligible for direct aid as independent states. The economy of each province, moreover, rests on the export of primary resources: copper, timber, oil and gas in the case of Irian; coffee and sandalwood in East Timor; oil and natural gas in Aceh. None has a significant market within Indonesia and none benefits significantly from funnelling its exports through Indonesian intermediaries: indeed, a major cause of regional dissatisfaction is the fact that it is not local people but rather officials and business people from other parts of Indonesia, primarily Java, who derive most benefit from the exploitation of the provinces' major exports.[7] For Aceh, the nearby Malaysian economy presents a powerful pole of attraction; for Irian Jaya, the prospect of dealing directly with Japanese investors is inevitably appealing; for East Timor, the adjacent Australian economy, at least in times of prosperity, offers an alternative to be imagined.

The secessionist movements, however, are most unlikely to succeed and it is even less likely that Indonesia will disintegrate. Rather, it suggests that regional politics will remain a significant factor in whatever political order emerges in post-Suharto Indonesia, and that the rhythm of regional politics will be tied not just to the policies emanating from Jakarta but to the broader economic pulses of the Asia–Pacific region.

7. Thus, for instance, in East Timor a thinly concealed monopoly in the hands of the local military controls the local coffee trade, while Irianese and Acehnese generally hold only unskilled, lowly-paid jobs in the oil, copper and natural gas industries.

Further Reading

CHAPTER 1. THE ORIGINS OF MODERN INDONESIA

An excellent introduction to the history of Southeast Asia, including Indonesia, is Nicholas Tarling (ed.) *The Cambridge History of Southeast Asia*, 2 vols (1992, Cambridge University Press, Cambridge). The classic history of the region, now rather dated but still of value, is Hall D G E 1968 *A History of South-east Asia* (2nd edn, Macmillan, London). A J S Reid, in his *Southeast Asia in the Age of Commerce 1450–1680* (1988. Yale University Press, New Haven, vol. 1: *The Lands Below the Winds*), takes a very wide view of history, and treats the region as one integrated by the patterns of trade flowing through the South China Sea. Merle Ricklefs' *A History of Modern Indonesia* (1993. 2nd edn, Macmillan, London) is a good overview of Indonesian history since the coming of Islam.

Two important studies of the early history of Indonesia by O W Wolters are *Early Indonesian Commerce* (1967. Cornell University Press, Ithaca) and *The Fall of Srivijaya in Malay History* (1970. Cornell University Press, Ithaca). The same author has explored interstate relations in early Southeast Asia in Wolters O W 1982 *History, Culture, and Region in Southeast Asian Perspective* (Institute of Southeast Asian Studies, Singapore). The political structure of the kingdom of Mataram is dealt with by Soemarsaid Moertono in *State and Statecraft in Old Java: A Study of the Later Mataram Period, 16th to 19th Century* (1981. Revised edn, Cornell Modern Indonesia Project, Ithaca; Monograph Series, publication 43). The best analysis of traditional concepts of power in Java is Anderson B R O'G 1972 The Idea of Power in Javanese Culture. In Holt C (ed.) *Culture and Politics in Indonesia* (Cornell University Press, Ithaca and London), pp. 1–69.

A classic study of colonial Indonesia, though one which explicitly deals with Dutch actors and interests rather than Indonesian ones, is J S Furnivall's *Netherlands India: A Study of Plural Economy* (1967. Reprint of 1939 edn; Cambridge University Press, Cambridge). One of the first scholars to try to see Indonesian history in its own terms, rather than simply as an adjunct to European – primarily Dutch – history was J C van Leur, a collection of whose essays was published posthumously in 1955. See *Indonesian Trade and Society. Essays in Asian Social and Economic History*, trans. J S Holmes and A van Marle (Van Hoeve, The Hague). An excellent study of the Dutch in one part of Indonesia is Taylor J G 1983 *The Social World of Batavia: European and Eurasian in Dutch Asia* (University of Wisconsin Press, Madison).

On the rise of nationalism generally, see B R O'G Anderson 1991 *Imagined Communities. Reflections on the Origin and Spread of Nationalism* (2nd edn Verso, London). Important studies dealing with Indonesian nationalism include: Dahm B 1969 *Sukarno and the Struggle for Indonesian Independence*, trans. M F Somers Heidhues (Cornell University Press, Ithaca); Ingleson J 1979 *Road to Exile. The Indonesian Nationalist Movement, 1927–1934* (Heinemann, Singapore; Asian Studies Association of Australia Southeast Asia Publications Series); Legge J D 1972 *Sukarno. A Political Biography* (Allen Lane The Penguin Press, London); Shiraishi T 1990 *An Age in Motion: Popular Radicalism in Java, 1912–1926* (Cornell University Press, Ithaca); van Niel R 1970 *The Emergence of the Modern Indonesian Elite* (van Hoeve, The Hague). A new translation of the collected letters of Raden Ajeng Kartini, a pioneer Indonesian feminist, by J J P Cote (ed. and trans.) is *Letters from Kartini: An Indonesian feminist, 1900–1904* (1992. Monash Asia Institute in association with Hyland House, Clayton). A useful collection of documents, though better for the study of Dutch colonialism than Indonesian nationalism, trans. and ed. C L M Penders, is *Indonesia. Selected Documents on Colonialism and Nationalism 1830–1942* (1977. University of Queensland Press, St Lucia).

The bias towards Java found in most studies of Indonesia during this period can be offset with Andaya L Y 1993 *The World of Maluku: Eastern Indonesia in the Early Modern Period* (University of Hawaii Press, Honolulu); Pelzer K J 1978 *Planter and Peasant: Colonial Policy and Agrarian Struggle in East Sumatra, 1863–1947* (KITLV, Leiden); Reid A J S 1969 *The Contest for North Sumatra: Atjeh, the Netherlands and Britain, 1858–1898* (Oxford University

Press, Kuala Lumpur) and Andaya L Y 1981 *The Heritage of Arung Palakka: A History of South Sulawesi (Celebes) in the Seventeenth Century* (Nijhoff, The Hague).

The Japanese occupation is covered well in Benda H J 1958 *The Crescent and the Rising Sun: Indonesian Islam under the Japanese Occupation, 1942–1945* (van Hoeve, The Hague) and Friend T 1988 *The Blue-eyed Enemy: Japan against the West in Java and Luzon, 1942–1945* (Princeton University Press, Princeton).

Four important novels which deal with the rise of Indonesian nationalism are by Pramoedya Ananta Toer, probably Indonesia's finest living writer. The books, all translated by Max Lane, are: *This Earth of Mankind* (1981. Penguin, Ringwood); *Child of All Nations* (1982. Penguin, Ringwood); *Footsteps* (1990. Penguin, Ringwood); *House of Glass* (1992. Penguin, Ringwood). For a critical survey of the development of Indonesian literature, see Teeuw A 1979–1986 *Modern Indonesian Literature*, 2 vols (2nd and 3rd edns, Nijhoff, The Hague).

A useful reference book, with an extensive bibliography, is Cribb R 1992 *Historical Dictionary of Indonesia* (Scarecrow, Metuchen and London).

CHAPTER 2. INDEPENDENCE UNDEFINED, 1945–49

For many years the standard work on Indonesia's war of independence and the associated social turmoil was Kahin G McT 1952 *Nationalism and Revolution in Indonesia* (Cornell University Press, Ithaca). As with its earlier section on the nationalist movement, however, much of the book has now been superseded by more detailed studies. The first reconsiderations of the independence war focused on the place of the Left: despite its title, McVey R T 1957 *The Soviet View of the Indonesian Revolution* (Cornell University Modern Indonesia Project, Ithaca; Interim Reports Series) dealt in greater details with the events leading to the Madiun Affair, as did Anderson D C 1976 'Military Aspects of the Madiun Affair'. *Indonesia* 21: 1–64. In contrast, Anderson B R O'G 1972 *Java in a Time of Revolution: Occupation and Resistance, 1944–1946* (Cornell University Press, Ithaca) brought to the fore the role of Tan Malaka and suggested that Sjahrir's preference for negotiations with the Dutch wasted an opportunity for thoroughgoing social revolution led by the central government. Reid A J S 1974 *The Indonesian National Revolution. 1945–1950*

(Longman, Hawthorn), which took account of these arguments, is now the standard text on the period, largely superseding Kahin's work.

Since Reid's volume appeared, study of the period has focused especially on events at the regional level. A number of such studies are summarised in Kahin A R (ed.) 1985 *Regional Dynamics of the Indonesian Revolution: Unity from Diversity* (University of Hawaii Press, Honolulu), but the full rich texture of events away from national-level politics is better examined in the full-length studies: see Chauvel R 1990 *Nationalists, Soldiers and Separatists* (Koninklijk Instituut voor Taal-, Land- en Volkenkunde, Leiden), (on Ambon); Cribb R B 1991 *Gangsters and Revolutionaries. The Jakarta People's Militia and the Indonesian Revolution 1945–1949* (Allen & Unwin, Sydney; Asian Studies Association of Australia, Southeast Asia Publications Series); Frederick W H 1988 *Visions and Heat: The Making of the Indonesian Revolution* (Ohio University Press, Athens), (on Surabaya); Lucas A 1991 *One Soul One Struggle. Region and Revolution in Indonesia* (Allen & Unwin, Sydney; Asian Studies Association of Australia, Southeast Asia Publications Series), (on the north coast of Central Java); Reid A J S 1979 *The Blood of the People: Revolution and the End of Traditional Rule in Northern Sumatra* (Oxford University Press, Kuala Lumpur). All these works show the complex way in which local issues intertwined with the nationalist struggle to produce distinctive local revolutions.

The war of independence has also attracted attention as the forge of the Indonesian army, with the origins of the army's political orientations being drawn out in particular in Sundhaussen U 1982 *The Road to Power: Indonesian Military Politics 1945–1967* (Oxford University Press, Kuala Lumpur) and Penders C L M and Sundhaussen U 1985 *Abdul Haris Nasution. A Political Biography* (University of Queensland Press, St Lucia). T B Simatupang's *Report from Banaran: The Story of the Experiences of a Soldier during the War of Independence* (1972. Cornell University Modern Indonesia Project. Ithaca; Translation Series) captures some of the atmosphere of the guerrilla struggle in the last months of the war, though Salim Said's *Genesis of Power. General Sudirman and the Indonesian Military in Politics 1945–49* (1991. Institute of Southeast Asian Studies, Singapore) and Cribb's *Gangsters and Revolutionaries*, which make closer use of documents of the time, cast doubts on some of the more exuberant military myths. The international relations of the time have been well covered in George M 1980 *Australia and the Indonesian Revolution* (Melbourne University

Press, Melbourne), McMahon R J 1981 *Colonialism and the Cold War: the United States and the Struggle for Indonesian Independence* (Cornell University Press, Ithaca) and Taylor A M 1960 *Indonesian Independence and the United Nations* (Cornell University Press, Ithaca). Surprisingly little attention has been paid by English-language authors to the evolving strategies of the Dutch during these crucial years, although Yong Mun Cheong makes an important start in *H J van Mook and Indonesian Independence* (1982. Nijhoff, The Hague).

CHAPTER 3. TOWARDS A UNITARY INDONESIA

Herbert Feith's *Decline of Constitutional Democracy in Indonesia* (1962. Cornell University Press, Ithaca) is still the standard work on Indonesia for the years from 1950 to 1957. His account of the destruction of federalism and the first regional rebellions has now been supplemented by Richard Chauvel 1990 *Nationalists, Soldiers and Separatists* (Koninklijk Instituut voor Taal-, Land- en Volkenkunde, Leiden). The politics of the separation of western New Guinea are discussed from an Indonesian point of view in Anak Agung Gde Agung 1973 *Twenty Years Indonesian Foreign Policy* (Mouton, The Hague) and from a Dutch point of view in Arendt Lijphart 1966 *The Trauma of Decolonisation* (Yale University Press, New Haven and London). Robert C Bone's *The Dynamics of the Western New Guinea (Irian Barat) Problem* (1958. Cornell Modern Indonesia Project, Ithaca; Interim Reports Series) is a useful academic survey. In *Central Authority and Regional Autonomy in Indonesia: A Study of Local Administration 1950–1960* (1961. Cornell University Press, Ithaca), John Legge offers considerable detail on the administrative structure of the unitary state, while Daniel Lev's 'The Politics of Judicial Unification in Indonesia' (1973. *Indonesia* 16: 1–38) focuses on internal legal aspects of the transition to independence.

Cees van Dijk's *Rebellion under the Banner of Islam* (1981. Nijhoff, The Hague; Verhandelingen van het Koninklijk Instituut voor Taal-, Land- en Volkenkunde) is the best study of the Darul Islam, though Boland's *The Struggle of Islam in Modern Indonesia* (2nd edn 1982, Martinus Nijhoff, The Hague) is also useful. Nazaruddin Syamsuddin 1985 *Republican Revolt* (Institute of Southeast Asian Studies, Singapore) is a detailed study of the rebellion in Aceh. The standard work on the Chinese during this period is Charles

Coppel 1983 *Indonesian Chinese in Crisis* (Oxford University Press, Kuala Lumpur; Asian Studies Association of Australia, Southeast Asia Publications Series). Richard Robison 1986 *Indonesia: The Rise of Capital* (Allen & Unwin, Sydney; Asian Studies Association of Australia, Southeast Asia Publications Series), discusses the Benteng programme.

CHAPTER 4. PARTY DOMINANCE, 1950–55

Feith's comprehensive study, *The Decline of Constitutional Democracy in Indonesia* (1962. Cornell University Press, Ithaca), remains the standard work on the years of party dominance in Indonesia. Unlike Kahin's study of nationalism and revolution, Feith's work did not form the basis for studies which amplified and modified its conclusions. Rather it was challenged almost immediately by the view that parliamentary democracy was alien and unsuited to Indonesia. This view, influentially expressed by Benda in his 'Democracy in Indonesia' (1964. *Journal of Asian Studies* 23: 449–56), effectively focused scholarly attention away from the 1950s and towards the more imaginative political experiments of Guided Democracy and the New Order. The inconsequentiality of the parliamentary system has also been stressed by Sundhaussen's more recent *Road to Power: Indonesian military politics 1945–1967* (1982. Oxford University Press, Kuala Lumpur).

Rocamora J E 1975 *Nationalism in Search of Ideology: the Indonesian National Party, 1946–1965)* (University of the Philippines, Quezon City), is a useful study of the PNI and is complemented by the memoirs of the party's longest serving prime minister, published as Ali Sastroamijoyo 1979 *Milestones on my Journey*, ed. C L M Penders (University of Queensland Press, St Lucia). A good study of the PKI is Hindley D 1964 *The Communist Party of Indonesia 1951–1963* (University of California Press, Berkeley and Los Angeles). Webb P R A F 1978 *Indonesian Christians and their Political Parties, 1923–1966* (James Cook University, Townsville) is indispensable on the Partai Katolik and Parkindo. The other parties have been less thoroughly studied, but Boland B J 1982, *The Struggle of Islam in Modern Indonesia* 2nd edn, (Martinus Nijhoff, The Hague) gives considerable attention to the Masjumi and Nahdatul Ulama and Burns P 1981 *Revelation and Revolution: Natsir and the Panca Sila* (Committee of Southeast Asian Studies, James Cook University, Townsville), offers the only detailed study of the

Masjumi's foremost political leader. Feith H and Castles L (eds) 1970 *Indonesian Political Thinking 1945–1965* (Cornell University Press, Ithaca), is a compendium of Indonesian writing on a variety of topics, much of it to do with the 1950s. McVey R T 1971a 'The Post-Revolutionary Transformation of the Indonesian Army' (*Indonesia* 11: 131–76) and 1971b 'The Post-Revolutionary Transformation of the Indonesian Army'. (*Indonesia* 13: 147–82) are useful adjuncts to Sundhaussen on military politics. Leifer M 1983 *Indonesia's Foreign Policy* (George Allen & Unwin, London, for the Royal Institute of International Affairs) is a standard work. On economic policy, Sutter J 1959 *Indonesianisasi: Politics of a Changing Economy* (Cornell University Department of Far Eastern Studies, Ithaca; Data Paper Series), is comprehensive but somewhat tedious. Robison 1986 *Indonesia: The Rise of Capital* (Allen and Unwin, Sydney; Asian Studies Association of Australia, Southeast Asia Publications Series), sets the economic policies of the 1950s in the broader context of Indonesia's capitalist development.

CHAPTER 5. BURYING THE PARTY SYSTEM, 1955–59

Feith H 1957 *The Indonesian Elections of 1955* (Cornell University Modern Indonesia Project, Ithaca), together with van Marle A 1956 'The First Indonesian Parliamentary Elections'. *Indonesië* 9: 257–64 are virtually the only serious studies of the only free general elections in Indonesian history, though they are also discussed in Feith H 1962 *Decline of Constitutional Democracy in Indonesia* (Cornell University Press, Ithaca), which outlines in detail the unravelling of the parliamentary system which followed the elections. Lev D 1966 *The Transition to Guided Democracy: Indonesian Politics, 1957–1979* (Cornell University Modern Indonesia Project, Ithaca; Interim Reports Series), picks up the story with the fall of the Ali cabinet and carries it through to mid-1959. Ghoshal B 1982 *Indonesian Politics 1955–59: The Emergence of Guided Democracy* (Bagchi, Calcutta), though not strongly analytical, is a useful alternative source on this period.

Reeve D 1985 *Golkar of Indonesia: An Alternative to the Party System* (Oxford University Press, Singapore), is a most important study of the functional group ideology which underpinned Guided Democracy, while Legge J D 1973 *Sukarno: A Political Biography* (Penguin, Harmondsworth) is useful on the president's position.

Sundhaussen U 1982 *Road to Power*, stresses the extent to which parliamentary democracy collapsed under the weight of its internal difficulties.

The rebellion in eastern Indonesia is described in some detail in Harvey B 1977 *Permesta: Half a Rebellion* (Cornell University Modern Indonesia Project, Ithaca; Interim Reports Series); Smail J R W 1968 'The military politics of North Sumatra: December 1956 – October 1957'. *Indonesia* 6: 128–87 analyses the early stages of the Sumatra rebellion, but there is still no full study of the PRRI affair. Mossman J 1961 *Rebels in Paradise: Indonesia's Civil War* (Jonathan Cape, London) is a useful discussion of life in the rebel areas.

CHAPTER 6. TOWARDS CATACLYSM, 1959–65

Although nowhere near as comprehensive as *Decline of Constitutional Democracy*, Feith H 1963 The Dynamics of Guided Democracy, in McVey R T (ed.) *Indonesia* (HRAF Press, New Haven) provides a good introduction to the period. There are several biographies of Sukarno, of which the best is Legge J D 1972 *Sukarno. A Political Biography* (Allen Lane The Penguin Press, London): the Guided Democracy period is dealt with in Chapters 11–15. A wide-ranging collection of essays on the period is Tan T K (ed.) 1967 *Sukarno's Guided Indonesia* (Jacaranda, Brisbane). Weatherbee D E 1966 *Ideology in Indonesia: Sukarno's Indonesian Revolution* (Yale University, Southeast Asian Studies, New Haven) is also useful.

Confrontation with Malaysia is covered exhaustively in Mackie J A C 1974 *Konfrontasi. The Indonesian–Malaysian Dispute 1963–1966* (Oxford University Press for the Australian Institute of International Affairs, Kuala Lumpur), and Sukarno's foreign policy in general in Leifer M 1983 *Indonesia's Foreign Policy* (George Allen & Unwin, London).

On the major political protagonists besides Sukarno, see Federspiel H M 1973 'The Military and Islam in Sukarno's Indonesia'. *Pacific Affairs* 46 (3): 407–20; Sundhaussen 1982 *Road to Power*; Mortimer R 1974 *Indonesian Communism under Sukarno: Ideology and Politics, 1959–1965* (Cornell University Press, Ithaca); Hindley D 1962 'President Sukarno and the Communists: the Politics of Domestication'. *American Political Science Review* 56 (4): 915–26; and Walkin J 1969 'The Muslim–Communist Confrontation in East Java, 1964–1965'. *Orbis* 13 (3): 822–47.

A good selection of contemporary writings about Guided Democracy by Indonesians, including Sukarno and Hatta, is Feith H and Castles L (eds) 1970 *Indonesian Political Thinking 1945–1965* (Cornell University Press, Ithaca), Chapter 3.

The extension of political conflict into the cultural arena is dealt with in Foulcher K 1986 *Social Commitment in Literature and the Arts: The Indonesian 'Institute of People's Culture', 1950–1965* (Monash University Centre of Southeast Asian Studies, Clayton).

CHAPTER 7. THE COUP, THE MASSACRES AND THE FALL OF SUKARNO, 1965–66

Crouch H 1978 *The Army and Politics in Indonesia* (Cornell University Press, Ithaca), provides the most balanced and dispassionate version of the events of 30 September and their aftermath. The New Order's version of the coup is set out in Nugroho Notosusanto and Saleh I 1968 *The Coup Attempt of the 'September 30 Movement' in Indonesia* (Pembimbing Masa, Jakarta). The first major account significantly questioning this version was Anderson B R O'G and McVey R T 1971 *A Preliminary Analysis of the October 1, 1965, Coup in Indonesia* (Cornell University Modern Indonesia Project, Ithaca; Interim Reports Series). The suspicions of Sukarno's involvement are discussed in Wertheim W F 1970 Suharto and the Untung coup – the missing link. *Journal of Contemporary Asia* 1 (2): 50–7. Sundhaussen 1982 *The Road to Power: Indonesian military politics 1945–1967* (Oxford University Press, Kuala Lumpur) offers many insights into the development of army politics over this period.

The human dimension of the aftermath of the coup is covered well in Cribb R (ed.) 1990 *The Indonesian Killings of 1965–1966* (Monash University Centre of Southeast Asian Studies, Clayton).

Unfortunately there is no critical biography of Suharto available.

CHAPTER 8. POLITICS SUSPENDED, 1966–73

For the early years of the New Order, Crouch H 1978 *The Army and Politics in Indonesia* (Cornell University Press, Ithaca), is still the best general survey, although McDonald H 1980 *Suharto's Indonesia* (Fontana, Melbourne), is also useful. Feith H 1968 Suharto's Search for a Political Format. *Indonesia* 6: 88–103 pays especial attention to Suharto's political decisions after the fall of

Sukarno. Oey H L (ed.) 1974 *Indonesia After the 1971 Elections* (Oxford University Press, London) is also useful.

Much has been written on the management of Indonesian elections. Crouch H 1971 The Army, the Parties and the Elections. *Indonesia* 11: 177–92; Nishihara M 1972 *Golkar and the Indonesian Elections of 1971* (Cornell University Modern Indonesia Project. Ithaca; Monograph Series) and Ward K E 1974 *The 1971 Election in Indonesia: an East Java Case Study* (Monash University Centre of Southeast Asian Studies, Clayton) are amongst the best. Thoolen H (ed.) 1987 *Indonesia and the Rule of Law: Twenty Years of 'New Order' Government* (Pinter, London) assesses the human rights record of the New Order.

The economic performance of the New Order can best be followed through the regular 'Survey of Recent Developments' published in the *Bulletin of Indonesian Economic Studies*, but Booth A and McCawley P (eds) 1981 *The Indonesian Economy during the Suharto Era* (Oxford University Press, Kuala Lumpur), is a valuable compendium. The Green Revolution receives competent treatment in Booth A 1988 *Agricultural Development in Indonesia* (Allen & Unwin, Sydney), while transmigration is discussed critically in Otten M 1986 *Transmigrasi, Myths and Realities: Indonesian resettlement policy, 1965–1985* (International Workshop for Indigenous Affairs, Copenhagen).

A valuable collection of theoretical discussions on Indonesian politics is Anderson B and Kahin A (eds) 1982 *Interpreting Indonesian Politics: Thirteen Contributions to the Debate* (Cornell University Modern Indonesia Project, Ithaca; Monograph Series).

CHAPTER 9. TOWARDS A CORPORATE STATE, 1974–87

The most comprehensive studies of Indonesian politics in this era are Vatikiotis M 1992 *Indonesian Politics under Suharto: order, development and pressure for change* (1993. revised edn, Routledge, London and New York) and Jenkins D 1984 *Suharto and his Generals: Indonesian Military Politics 1975–1983* (Cornell University Modern Indonesia Project, Ithaca; Monograph Series). Three recent and very useful studies are Bresnan J 1993 *Managing Indonesia: The Modern Political Economy* (Columbia University Press, New York and London), Hill H (ed.) 1994 *Indonesia's New Order: The Dynamics of Socio-economic Transformation* (Allen & Unwin, Sydney) and Schwarz A 1994 *A Nation in Waiting: Indonesia in the 1990s* (Allen & Unwin, Sydney) McDonald H 1980 *Suharto's Indonesia* (Fontana, Melbourne) remains useful for the early years.

Three articles have been especially important in shaping academic understanding of the high New Order; they are Anderson B R O'G 1983 'Old State, New Society: Indonesia's New Order in Comparative Historical Perspective'. *Journal of Asian Studies* 42 (3): 477–98; Emmerson D K 1983 'Understanding the New Order: Bureaucratic Pluralism in Indonesia'. *Asian Survey* 23 (11): 1220–41; and Liddle W R 1985 'Suharto's Indonesia: Personal Rule and Political Institutions.' *Pacific Affairs* 58 (1): 68–90.

Bourchier D 1984 *Dynamics of Dissent in Indonesia: Sawito and the Phantom Coup* (Cornell University Modern Indonesia Project, Ithaca; Interim Reports Series) and Burns P 1989 'The Post Priok Trials: Religious Principles and Legal Issues'. *Indonesia* 47: 61–88 discuss the regime's management of dissent.

Gunn G C 1979 'Ideology and the Concept of Government in the Indonesian New Order'. *Asian Survey* 19 (8): 751–69 and Morfit M 1981 'Pancasila: the Indonesian state ideology according to the New Order'. *Asian Survey* 21 (8): 838–51, offer careful considerations of the Pancasila as it was employed by the Indonesian government in these years. Bowen J R 1986 'On the Political Construction of Tradition: *gotong royong* in Indonesia'. *Journal of Asian Studies* 45 (3): 545–61, shows how the ideology of the Pancasila is also applied to daily life, especially in rural Indonesia.

Dwifungsi, its ideological basis and consequences are discussed in MacDougall J A 1982 'Patterns of Military Control in the Indonesian Higher Central Bureaucracy'. *Indonesia* 33: 89–121; and Sundhaussen, U 1980 *Social Policy Aspects in Defence and Security Planning in Indonesia, 1947–1977* (James Cook University, Townsville).

A good early discussion of developments in Timor is Nicol B 1978 *Timor. The Stillborn Nation* (Visa, Melbourne). Very critical of Indonesia is Budiardjo C and Liem S L 1984 *The War Against East Timor* (Zed, London). A useful review of Indonesian policies in East Timor was undertaken by a team of highly respected academics from Gadjah Mada University in Yogyakarta. The report, guardedly critical but with proposals for policy improvements, has been translated as Mubyarto, Loekman S et al. 1991 *East Timor: The Impact of Integration* (Indonesian Resources and Information Program, Melbourne).

CHAPTER 10. SOCIAL CHANGE AND FUTURE PROSPECTS

A number of annual publications sum up recent developments in Indonesian politics and provide early academic assessments on the significance of events. The Far Eastern Economic Review *Asia Yearbook* is especially useful, as is the annual Indonesia article in *Asian Survey*. Singapore's Institute of Southeast Asian Studies (ISEAS) publishes *Southeast Asian Affairs*, which focuses on selected themes in recent development. The *Bulletin of Indonesian Economic Studies* provides a regular Survey of Recent Developments, while for several years now the proceedings of the annual Indonesia Update, held at the Australian National University, have been published as *Indonesia Assessment*.

For an optimistic view of the capacity of local social ideas to withstand the conformist pressure of Pancasila, see Warren C 1990 'Rhetoric and resistance: popular political culture on Bali'. *Anthropological Forum* 6 (2): 191–205.

Cushman J and Wang Gungwu (eds) 1988 *Changing Identities of the Southeast Asian Chinese since World War II* (Hong Kong University Press, Hong Kong) has several useful chapters on the Chinese in Indonesia.

Budiman A (ed.) 1990 *State and Civil Society in Indonesia* (Monash Papers on Southeast Asia, Clayton) and Bourchier D and Legge J (eds) 1994 *Democracy in Indonesia: 1950s and 1990s* Monash University Centre of Southeast Asian Studies, Clayton) are both good collections of articles on contemporary Indonesia.

A good introduction to the study of the emerging Indonesian middle class is Tanter R and Young K (eds) 1990 *The Politics of Middle-Class Indonesia* (Monash University Centre of Southeast Asian Studies, Clayton).

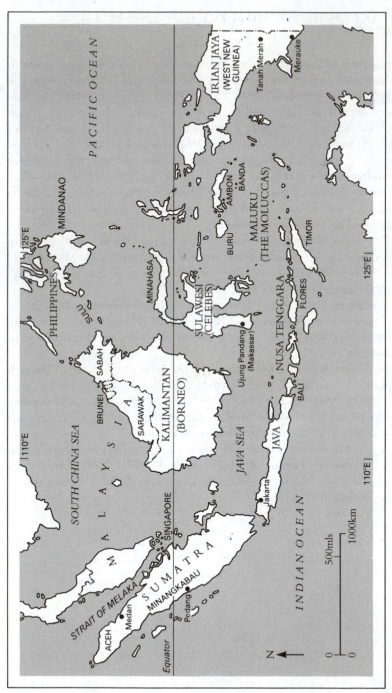

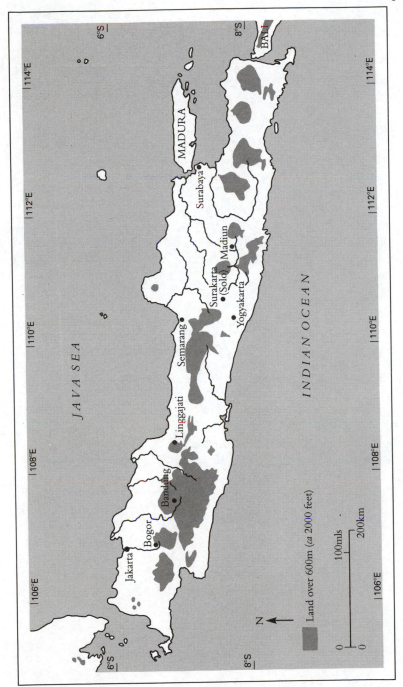

6°S

8°S

BALI

114°E

112°E

MADURA

Surabaya

Madiun

Surakarta
(Solo)

Yogyakarta

Semarang

Linggajati

Bandung

Bogor

Jakarta

110°E

108°E

106°E

J A V A   S E A

I N D I A N   O C E A N

N

Land over 600m (*ca* 2000 feet)

0   100mls

0   200km

6°S

8°S

Java

Index